~Don't Stop The~ Party!

A Complete Guide to Tropical Drink Recipes

· Part One ·

Over 1,001 Cocktail, Shooter,
Frozen and Flame Drink Recipes from the
Florida Keys, Bahamas and all
the Caribbean Islands.

by PostCard USA

This Book Was Pirated By:

_____

Keep Your Hands Off!
Get Your Own Copy!

Special Thanks

Many thanks to everybody who had input in making this book.
To compile all the recipes and to put the book together was a lot of fun, and at times also frustrating. Some of the drinks have names which might be offensive to some readers. We debated some of the Drink Recipe Titles, and eliminated what we thought were not appropriate. On the other hand we did not want to eliminate the real good stuff. I think we found a healthy, sexy medium.

Don't Stop The Party

Published by Pro Publishing, Inc.
www.BlueWaterIslands.com
SW Ranches, FL 33331, Florida
© 2003 by Pro Publishing, Inc.

Printed and Designed by www.PostCardusa.com
PCUSA 2518

Printed in Korea

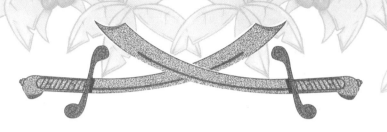

Pirates, Buccaneers, and Privateers

Piracy is the crime of robbery or an act of violence for private gain on the high sea. It is committed by the captain and/or their crew outside the normal jurisdiction of any nation or without any authority from any government. The people who engage in these acts are called "Pirates." Legislation and treaties between countries have sometimes applied the term "piracy" in order to attack high sea ships legally, and with authorization by a government. Such acts however, were not regarded as piracy under the law of nations. Those were called "privateering," as it was acting for a political purpose. This was officially abolished by the Declaration of Paris in 1856. The United States and other nations did not follow this declaration.

Piracy has existed for a long time. Phoenicians combined piracy with their usual seafaring business. European coast lines were terrorized by the Vikings from the 9th through the 11th century.
A Hanseatic group was formed in the 13th century to create a mutual defense against pirates roaming the North and Baltic Sea. In the Mediterranean Sea, Muslim ships scoured for loot and slaves. Then in the 17th century, Algerian pirates operated out of northern Africa all the way up the English Channel. Algiers was the pirates stronghold into the mid 19th century.

The laws, in terms of piracy, have been revised and extended to include crimes such as slave trading. Every independent state has the power and can regulate its own criminal laws to declare offenses to be piracy that usually are not considered such by international laws. These local laws can only be enforced in the jurisdiction that created them. Similar regulations and laws may be adopted by other states without a special agreement between those states. The officers of one state may not arrest or punish pirates or offenses committed outside their jurisdiction.

"**Buccaneer**" was an official title for English, Dutch, and French seafarers of the 17th century. Daring seaman such as Englishmen Sir Francis Drake and Sir Richard Hawkins became wealthy in operations against Spain. Those men were lured by the riches of the merchant ships mostly in the Caribbean Sea and off the coast of North America. They harassed Spanish ships and colonies in the New World, mainly during the second half of the 17th century.

The most famous buccaneer, Sir Henry Morgan, was born in England. Privateers and buccaneers were different. They had official government commissions. Buccaneers rarely had such a commission. Also, pirates attacked ships of all nations, privateers only what the government decided.

The name "buccaneer" came from the practice of raiding Hispanola and stealing cattle from the plantations. They dried the meat on grills in a process called "boucan" by the French, and then sold to vessels. Later, the buccaneers used Jamaica as a base operation. With their leader, Captain Morgan, they captured Panama in 1671. The era came to an end in the early 18th century. Buccaneers were then hired by their governments to fight privateers in the War of the Spanish Succession between 1701 and 1714.

"**Privateer**" is the term applied to a privately owned ship with a commission of a hostile nation to initiate naval warfare. It is called "marque." Privateering is different from piracy which is carried out without the consent of a government. It was abolished by the "Declaration of Paris" in 1856, but the United States did not support it. Under the U.S. Constitution, Congress had the power to issue "letters of marque." It was carried out during the American Revolution and the War of 1812.

Fifteen men on a dead man's chest
> **Yo, ho, ho, and a bottle of rum**

Drink and the devil had done for the rest
> **Yo, ho, ho, and a bottle of rum.**

-Robert Louis Stevenson, *Treasure Island* 1883

Blackbeard

While in the Bahamas, Edward Teach began his odyssey as the most feared pirate on the high seas and came to acquire the ship he renamed "The Queen Anne's Revenge."

In New Providence, Teach met Capt. Benjamin Hornigold whose crew he joined in 1716. Shortly thereafter, he became Hornigold's protégé, and soon was given a captured sloop with six cannons to command while still serving under Hornigold.

It was during the latter part of 1717 that Hornigold and Teach encountered a large ship off St. Vincent flying the French flag. Hornigold and Teach both fired from their sloops across the bow of the French boat and killed many on board. The ship, known as the "Concorde" surrendered. She was actually a Dutch built 'flute' that had come into the possession of a St. Malo Frenchman. The boat was rich in booty, and with Hornigold's hold now filled with treasure, Teach asked if he could be given the command of the captured ship. Hornigold knew he was reaching the end of his pirating days, and with the wealth he had accumulated, he could retire. He agreed to give the ship to Teach and would retire to New Providence. It was the last time he would see the man he had trained well to become the vicious pirate, Blackbeard.

Blackbeard honed his piracy skills, selecting bigger and better targets. But his greatest feat was yet to come. In May 1718, Blackbeard decided to blockade the harbor of Charleston, South Carolina. He stretched his vessels across the harbor and made demands on the town for money, supplies and medicine. The blockade wore on for weeks, and without firing a shot, Blackbeard slowly received what he came for.

The humiliation of the town at the hands of pirates made the citizens determined to stop piracy and send a message to any who practiced it. Four months later, they got their hands on Stede Bonnet, Blackbeard's sometimes pirate friend. The people of Charleston hanged him.

Blackbeard gave his new ship the name "The Queen Anne's Revenge." He sailed the vessel until June of 1718, when he sailed it into the Beaufort Inlet, also known at that time as the Topsail Inlet. It was there that he intentionally ran the ship aground under the pretense of cleaning off the hull. In reality, he was plotting yet another theft of booty, but this time it was from his own crew and his then ally Stede Bonnett. He took the treasure, his favorite crew members and abandoned the ship in the inlet so it would be taken by the tide.

After abandoning "The Queen Anne's Revenge" and the smaller vessel "Adventure" in the inlet, Blackbeard and the remaining crew took the other ships up Pamlico Sound to the town of Bath. There he received a pardon from the Royal Governor and lived for a time making friends with the locals and the wealthy planters.

The lure of piracy was too much for Edward Teach, and he soon fell back into sailing the North Carolina and Virginia Coast looking for ships to plunder. He had settled on Ocracoke Island, near Cape Hatteras, as his outpost. It was here that Lieutenant Maynard of the Royal Navy found Blackbeard anchored at his favorite spot on the south side of the island. His ships crept up on Blackbeard's and a fierce battle broke out between them. Both sides took heavy casualties, and eventually Blackbeard was killed in battle. He was overwhelmed by the training and firepower of the Royal Navy. Blackbeard's head was cut off and his body thrown overboard where legend tells that it swam around the ship several times before sinking. The skull was displayed as a trophy on Maynard's arrival in Bath and in Virginia.

Setting Up a Bar

Nowadays people are drinking less alcohol and you will need more wine and beer, bottled water and soft drinks than hard liquor. Don't buy out the whole liquor store when you go shopping. Only choose what your guests will drink. If you are not sure, just take the basics: vodka, gin, whiskey, scotch, tequila, rum, vermouth, beer and wine.

Plenty of mixers like tonic water, coke, orange, grapefruit, tomato and cranberry juice, ginger ale and carbonated water will be helpful. Have a variety of nonalcoholic drinks for nondrinkers: Sodas, vegetable and fruit juice, water, iced tea, tea and coffee. Many guests will drink alcoholic as well as nonalcoholic beverages.

Buy garnish for cocktails such us cherries and olives, limes and lemons. Don't forget the ice! You should have at least one pound of ice cubes per person for longer parties, parties on hot days, or parties on the beach.
It is not necessary to have a wide selection of glasses. Twelfe ounce glasses and stemmed wine glasses will work for almost every drink. However, if you prefer you can buy or rent tulip glasses, shooters, martini and other glasses needed.
Be sure you have a bottle opener, corkscrew, napkins, small towels as well as a wastebasket handy. A blender will also serve well for blended drink such as margaritas or daiquiris.
It is always a good idea to set up the bar seperate from the food table. Make it self-serve or have a friend to act as a bartender.

Overview of Bartending

• ½ oz. of liquor is equivalent to 1 count. If you have a pourer on the bottle, to gauge 1 ½ oz. of liquor, count "1001…1002…1003" while pouring. With experience, you will be able to measure by sight.
• Highballs: Fill a highball glass two-thirds full with ice prior to adding liquor. Always pour liquor first, then the mixer. Drinks containing a mixer with carbonation should not be stirred.
• Cocktails: (Lowballs and other stirred or shaken drinks) Fill a shaker half-full with ice. When serving a lowball drink, fill the glass approximately half-full with ice prior to pouring drink.
• Drinks containing light cream can also be prepared as a blended drink by omitting the light cream and substituting vanilla ice cream.
• Blended drinks: Fill a blender half-full with ice. If needed, add more ice as drink is blending.
• Always refrigerate fruit juices and mixers.
• Always use fruit that is fresh in fruit drinks: never frozen.

Beer & Wine Servicing

Draft Beer Service
• Deliver immediately after beer is ordered and poured.
• As you pour beer, tilt the beer mug allowing a 1-inch head to develop on top of beer.
The head not only enhances its appearance, but the taste also.
• A "perfect pour" is not one without foam.

Bottled Beer Service
• Always inquire if they desire a mug.
• Always open the bottle of beer for guests.
• Always present the bottle with label facing the guest.
• If guests want a mug, offer to pour it for them (only pour approximately ½ full).

Wine Service
• Just like beer, wine should be served at once.
• Always open the bottle in front of guests after they inspect the label.
• It is not proper to smell the cork.
• Giving a small taste to guests is appropriate only in restaurants, but not at home.
• Pour carefully, so not to touch the bottle to the wine glass.
• Fill a wine glass only 2/3 full (twist the wine bottle slightly at end of pouring to prevent drips).

Glasses to Use for Different Types of Drinks

- 14 oz Collins Glass
    - Soft Drinks
    - Alcoholic Juice Drinks
    - Collins
    - Sours
    - Bloody Mary
- 8 oz Highball
    - Bourbon/Ginger
    - White Russian
- 4 ½ oz Rocks
    - Chilled Shooters
    - Single Shots
- 6 oz Cocktail Glass
    - Martinis
    - Any chilled "up" drinks
- 8 oz Wine Glass
    - Wine
    - Champagne
- 12 ½ oz Tall Wine
    - Frozen Drinks
    - Ice Cream Drinks
    - Tropical Drinks
    - Mimosas
    - Daiquiris
    - Margaritas

- 2 oz Sherry Glass
    - Liqueurs
    - Layered Shooters
    - Ports
- 17 ½ oz Snifter
    - Brandies
    - Cognacs
- 8 ½ oz Footed Mug
    - All Hot drinks

Jigger Amounts
A jigger consists of two sides – 1 ¼ oz and ¾ oz.

For a:
- 1 ¼ oz pour – use 1 ¼ oz side
- ¾ oz pour – use ¾ oz side
- ½ oz pour – eyeball using ¾ oz side
- 1 oz pour – eyeball using 1 ¼ oz side
- 1 ½ oz pour – use ¾ oz side twice
- 2 oz pour – use 1 ¼ oz & ¾ oz together

Always pour light liquors before any liqueurs. Liqueurs are heavier causing the flavor to possibly adhere to the jigger. When pouring numerous drinks, line the glasses up collectively and hold the jigger by the rear of glass. This allows you to move more quickly and to have better control of the bottle. Always rinse a jigger after using a liqueur. Place the jigger on its side after use in order to allow any excess to drain. When possible, acquire a spill mat: this is a necessity for serious bartenders.

1 Tulip   **2** Cocktail Glass   **3** Shooter   **4** Irish Coffee Mug   **5** Cordial   **6** Champagne Flute

7 Wine Goblet   **8** Rocks/Old Fashion   **9** Sherry Glass   **10** Highball Glass   **11** Snifter   **12** Beer Mug

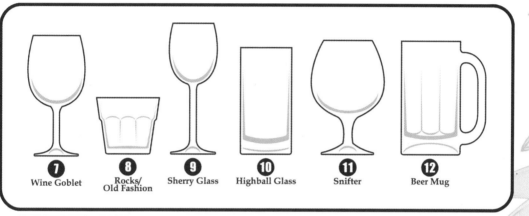

13 Punch Cup   **14** Daiquiri   **15** Margarita   **16** Martini   **17** Pony   **18** Hurricane

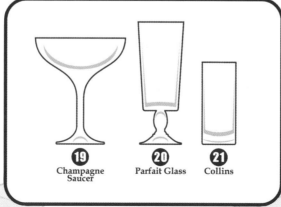

19 Champagne Saucer   **20** Parfait Glass   **21** Collins

CHARTS

Standard Bar Measurements

Measurement	Metric Equivalent	Standard Equivalent
1 dash	0.9 ml	1/32 oz.
1 teaspoon	3.7 ml	1/8 oz.
1 tablespoon	11.1 ml	3/8 oz.
1 pony	29.5 ml	1 oz.
1 jigger	44.5 ml	1 1/2oz.
1 miniature	59.2 ml	2 oz.
1 wine glass	119.0 ml	4 oz.
1 split	177.0 ml	6 oz.
1 half pint	257.0 ml	8 oz.
1 tenth	378.88 ml	12.8 oz.
1 "pint"(1/2 bottle wine)	375.2 ml	12 oz.
1 pint	472.0 ml	16 oz.

Bottle Sizes

Miniature	50 ml	1.7 oz
Split	187 ml	6.3 oz
1/2 Pint	200 ml	6.8 oz
Tenth	375 ml	12.7 oz
Pint	500 ml	16.9 oz
Fifth	750 ml	25.4 oz
Quart	1 liter	33.8 oz
Magnum	1.5 L	50.7 oz
Half Gallon	1.75 L	59.2 oz
Jeroboam	3 liters	101.4 oz

Measurements

1 Dash	1/32 oz.
1 Teaspoon	1/8 oz.
1 Tablespoon	3/8 oz.
1 Pony	1 oz.
1 Jigger	1 1/2 oz.
1 Wine Glass	4 oz.
1 Split	6 oz.
1 Cup	8 oz.

CHARTS

US / Metric Conversion

1 Ounce	=	29.537 ML
1 Quart	=	.946 L
1 Gallon	=	3.785 L
1.381 Ounces	=	1 ML
10.58 Quarts	=	1 L
.246 Gallons	=	1 L

Drink Chart

Body Weight	Number of Drinks in One Hour					
	1	2	3	4	5	6
100	.038	.075	.113	.150	.188	.225
120	.031	.063	.094	.125	.156	.188
140	.027	.054	.080	.107	.134	.161
160	.023	.047	.070	.094	.17	.141
180	.021	.042	.063	.083	.104	.124
200	.019	.038	.056	.075	.094	.13
220	.017	.034	.051	.068	.085	.102
240	.016	.031	.047	.063	.078	.094

Blood Alcohol Level (BAC)

Impaired DO NOT DRIVE	Intoxicated DO NOT DRIVE

This is a guide only. Food consumption, medication and other physical conditions may vary these figures.

One drink is one shot of 80 proof liquor, 12 oz beer, or 4 oz wine

MAP OF THE
WEST INDIES
AND THE
CARIBBEAN

ATLANTIC OCEAN

BAHAMAS

DOR

CAY

Mayaguana

TURKS & CAICOS ISLANDS

AGUA

LEEWARD ISLANDS

HISPANIOLA

Labadee
Port de Paix
Cap Haïtien
Puerto Plata
Santiago
HAITI
DOMINICAN REPUBLIC
Port au Prince
Bani
Santo Domingo
La Romana
Jaemel
Barahona

VIRGIN IS.
Anegada
St.John
St.Thomas
B.V.I.
San Juan
PUERTO RICO
Ponce
Tortola
Virgin Gorda
Culebra
Vieques
St.Croix

ANGUILLA
ST.MARTIN/ST.MAARTEN
ST.BARTS

BARBUDA

ST. CHRISTOPHER
ST. KITTS
St.John
ANTIGUA
NEVIS
MONTSERRAT
GUADELOUPE
Pointe-a-Pitre
WINDWARD ISLANDS
Portsmouths
Roseau
Marigot
DOMINICA
Fort de France
MARTINIQUE
Castries
ST. LUCIA
Bridgetown
ST. VINCENT
BARBADOS

ANTILLES

BBEAN SEA

LESSER ANTILLES

The Grenadines

NETHERLANDS ANTILLES

ARUBA
Oranjestad
CURACAO
Willemstad
BONAIRE
Kralendijk

Roques Is.
Orchila
Blanquilla Is.

GRENADA
St.George
TOBAGO

Paraguana Peninsula
Cora

Margarita Is.
Los Testigos
Portamar
Port of Spain
Arima

nta Marta

Tortuga

Carapano
San Fernando
TRINIDAD

Maracaibo
Cabimas

Carora

Barquisimento

Puerto Cabello
San Felipe
Valencia
Maracaibo
Caracas
Los Teques

Grumau
Barcelona
Caripito
Maturia

Lake Maracaibo

San Juan

San Carlos

Valle

Trajillo
Valera
Guanare

V E N E Z U E L A

Cucuta
San Cristoba
Merida
Barinas
San Fernando
Ciudad Bolivar

~Don't Stop The~ Party!

A Complete Guide to Tropical Drink Recipes

· Part Two ·

The Recipes

A.S.S.

1/3 oz. Vodka   1/3 oz. Spearmint
1/3 oz. Sambuca

Put into a shot glass in the order given.

A-Bomb

1 1/2 oz. Gin   1 oz. Benedictine
1 splash Curaçao

Build over ice in an old fashioned glass.

Absinthe Cocktail

1 1/2 oz. Absinthe   1/2 oz. Anisette
1/2 oz. Water   1 dash Orange Bitters

Shake with ice and strain into a chilled cocktail glass.

Absinthe Curaçao Frappe

1 oz. Absinthe   1/2 oz. Curaçao
1 tsp. Lemon Juice 2 tsp. Orange Juice
1 slice Orange

Stir ingredients and pour over crushed ice. Add orange slice.

Absolut Sex

1/2 oz. Absolut Kurant 1/2 oz. Melon Liqueur
1/2 oz. Cranberry Juice 1/2 oz. 7-Up

Mix and pour in a glass over cubed ice.

Absolut Stress

1 oz. Absolut Vodka   1 oz. Malibu Rum
1/2 oz. Peach Schnapps 3 oz. Cranberry Juice
3 oz. Orange Juice   3 oz. Pineapple Juice

Mix liquors in shaker and strain, then add cranberry, orange and pineapple juices.

Absolute Bitch

1/2 oz. Absolut Vodka 1/4 oz. Bailey's
1/4 oz. Kahlua   1/4 oz. Tuaca

Shake with ice and strain into a shot glass.

Absolutely Blue Vodka Freeze

1 bottle Pepsi Blue   1 cup Absolut Vodka
1 cup Ice Cubes

Blend Pepsi Blue and ice cubes until slushy add 1 cup of Absolut Vodka.

Absolutely Crushed

4 whole Kumquats   2 whole Passion Fruits
2 oz. Absolut Citron   2 oz. Passoa
2 cups crushed Ice   1 Tbsp. Raw Sugar

Slice passion fruit and put seeds in a high ball glass. Slice kumquats and crush together with sugar and passion fruit. Add crushed ice. Pour Absolut Citron over ice and stir. Add more crushed ice then passoa.

Absolution

1 part Absolut Vodka   5 parts Champagne

Add ingredients in a fluted champagne glass. Cut a lemon peel in the shape of a ring to represent a halo. Wrap around the top of the glass.

Acapulco

1 1/2 oz. Tequila   1/2 oz. Light Rum
1/2 oz. Triple Sec   1 oz. Sour Mix
1 splash Lime Juice

Shake with ice and strain into an ice filled double old fashioned glass.

Admiral Cocktail

2 oz. Gin   3/4 oz. Lime Juice
1/2 oz. Peter Heering

Mix with cracked ice in a shaker. Strain into chilled cocktail glass.

Admiral Highball

1 1/2 oz. Bourbon   1 1/2 oz. Tokay Wine
7-UP
1 dash Lemon Juice & Pineapple Juice

Mix in a highball glass. Add ice and fill with 7-UP.

Adonis

1 1/2 oz. Dry Sherry   3/4 oz. Sweet Vermouth
1 dash Orange Bitters

Stir with ice and strain into a chilled cocktail glass.

Affair

1 oz. Cranberry Juice   1 oz. Orange Juice
1 oz. Strawberry Schnapps

Mix with ice and strain into a cordial glass.

Affinity Cocktail

1 oz. Scotch   1 oz. Dry Sherry
1 oz. Sweet Vermouth
2 dashes Angostura Bitters

Blend ingredients. Serve over cracked ice or strain to serve straight up.

After Burner

1/2 oz. Aftershock   1/2 oz. Bacardi Rum 151

Shake with ice and strain into a shot glass.

After Dinner Cocktail

1 oz. Apricot Brandy   1 oz. Triple Sec
3/4 oz. Lime Juice

Shake with ice and strain into cocktail glass. Garnish with lime twist.

After Eight

1/3 oz. Kahlua
1/3 oz. Green Crème de Menthe
1/3 oz. Irish Coffee Liqueur

Layer in order given in a shot glass.

After Five Shooter

1/2 oz. Peppermint Schnapps
1 oz. Coffee Liqueur

Mix ingredients with ice. Strain and pour into shot glass.

Afterburn

1 oz. Vodka   1/2 oz. Tabasco Sauce

Put in a shot glass. (Try at your own risk!)

① Aida's Frozen Delight

1/2 oz. Bailey's   Powdered Chocolate
3 scoops Vanilla Ice Cream
Whipped Cream

Combine and blend until smooth. Top with whipped cream and powdered chocolate.

---

② Alexander Cocktail

1 oz. Gin   1 oz. Cream
1 oz. White Crème de Cacao
1 sprinkle Nutmeg

Shake with ice and strain into chilled cocktail glass. Garnish with a sprinkle of nutmeg.

---

⑲ Alfonso

1 oz. Dubbonet   1 dash Angostura bitters
1 Sugar Cube   Chilled Champagne

Place sugar in a chilled champagne saucer glass and sprinkle with bitters. Add one ice cube, fill with champagne and garnish with a lemon twist.

---

③ Alien Secretion Shooter

1/2 oz. Midori   1/2 oz. Malibu Rum
1 splash Pineapple Juice

Shake with ice. Strain into a shot glass.

---

⑧ Almond Delight

1 oz. Amaretto   1 oz. Sambuca

Serve over ice.

㉑ Amarreto Cherry Sour

2 oz. Amaretto   5 oz. Sour Mix
5 oz. Cherry Juice

Fill a glass with ice. Pour ingredients and top with 2 cherries.

---

⑥ Ambrosia

1 oz. Apple Jack   1 oz. Brandy
1/4 oz. Cointreau   Lemon Juice
Champagne

Shake the first four ingredients over ice and strain into a champagne flute. Fill with champagne.

---

⑥ Americana I

1 tsp. Bourbon   1 dash Angostura Bitters
4 oz. Champagne   Fresh Peach slice

Pour the bourbon and bitters into a flute. Add champagne and garnish with the peach slice.

---

⑥ Americana II

1/2 tsp. Sugar   1-2 dashes Bitters
Champagne   1 Peach Slice
1/4 oz. George Dickel No. 12 Tennessee Whisky

Combine the whisky, bitters and sugar. Stir until the sugar is dissolved. Add champagne and a slice of peach.

---

② Anal Probe

1 oz. Spiced Rum   5 1/2 oz. Kahlua
2 oz. Cola   2 cups cracked Ice

Mix liquors in shaker with cracked ice. Put into chilled cocktail glass. Add cola.

---

⑦ Angel

1 oz. Bailey's   2/3 oz. Cointreau
1 oz. Cream   4 Strawberries
2/3 oz. Strawberry Liqueur
1 oz. Pineapple Juice

Combine with ice in blender. Pour into a large goblet.

Angelic

8
2

1 oz. Bourbon 2 oz. Half & Half
1/2 oz. White Crème de Cacao
dash Grenadine

Shake with ice and serve on rocks or stain into cocktail glass.

Angel's Delight

3

1/4 oz. Triple Sec 1/4 oz. Crème Yvette
1/4 oz. Grenadine 1/4 oz. Cream

Slowly add grenadine to Triple Sec, Crème Yvette and cream (in exact order) into a tipped glass, so that liqueurs float on each other.

Angel's Kiss

3

1 1/2 oz. Dark Crème de Cacao
1/2 oz. Cream

Layer in exact order.

Angel's Wings

3

1/2 oz. Crème de Violette
1/2 oz. Maraschino
1/2 oz. Raspberry Syrup

Pour crème, raspberry syrup and maraschino (exact order) into tipped glass so that they float on each other.

Angle Piss

2

1 1/2 oz. Scotch 2 oz. Perrier
1 wedge Lime 1/2 cup Ice

Stir in mixing glass. Strain into chilled cocktail glass.

Angler's Cocktail

2

1 1/2 oz. Dry Gin 1 dash Grenadine
2 dashes Angostura Bitters
2 dashes Orange Bitters

Combine with ice and shake. Strain and add ice.

Anti-Freeze

2

1 dash 7-UP 1 oz. Blue Curaçao
1/2 oz. Spearmint Schnapps

Mix in a shaker with ice. Strain into a chilled cocktail glass.

Aperitivo Cocktail

2

1 1/2 oz. Dry Gin 1 oz. Sambuca
3 dashes Orange Bitters

Mix with cracked ice. Strain into chilled cocktail glass.

Aphrodite's Love Potion

10

1 Orange slice 1 Maraschino Cherry
4-5 oz. Pineapple Juice 1 1/2 oz. Metaxa Brandy
1-2 dashes Angostura Bitters

Mix into a tall glass with 4-5 ice cubes. Garnish with orange slice and cherry.

Apple Blow

2

1 1/2 oz. Applejack 1 Tbsp. Lemon Juice
1 Egg White 1 tsp. Superfine Sugar
1 oz. Apple Juice 6 oz. Club Soda

Mix ingredients in a shaker. Strain into a cocktail glass over ice.

Apple Colada

1

1 oz. Apple Schnapps 1/2 oz. Light Rum
2 splashes Cream 1 Cherry
3 splashes Pineapple Juice
2 splashes Cream of Coconut

Combine with crushed ice and blend until smooth. Garnish with cherry.

Apple Pucker

1 oz. Vodka   1 slice Lemon
1 oz. Green Apple Pucker
1 big dash Sprite

Combine all in shaker over ice. Mix and pour into chilled highball glass.

Apricot Lady

1 oz. Apricot Brandy   1 1/2 oz. White Rum
1/2 tsp. Curaçao   1 tsp. Lime Juice
1 Egg White   1 slice Orange

Combine with ice and shake. Strain over crushed ice. Garnish with fruit.

Aquarius

1/2 oz. Cherry Brandy   1 oz. Cranberry Juice
1 1/2 oz. Blended Whiskey

Build over ice in a lowball glass.

Around The World

1 dash Vodka   1 dash Rum
1 dash Gin   1 dash Tequila
1 dash Triple Sec   1 dash Peach Schnapps
1 dash Midori   1 dash Blue Curacao
1 dash 151 Rum   1 dash Amaretto
1 dash Malibu   1 dash Chambord
Sour Mix   Orange Juice
Pineapple Juice   Cranberry Juice
Sprite
1 dash Southern Comfort

Fill glass with cracked ice. Add alcohol and even parts sour mix, orange, pineapple, and cranberry juices and Sprite. Serve in tall glass.

Aruba

1 1/2 oz. Gin   1/2 oz. White Curaçao
1 oz. Lemon Juice   1/2 Egg White
1 tsp. Orgeat Syrup

Mix with ice in shaker. Strain into a cocktail glass.

Arubian Kiss

1 oz. Vodka   3/4 oz Malibu Rum
3/4 oz. Banana Liqueur   2 dashes Blue Curaçao
1 oz. Sour Mix   3 oz. Pineapple Juice

Shake, strain into a collins glass with ice.

Ass Kicker

2 oz. Goldschlager   2 oz. Rumplemintz
2 oz. Tequila   2 oz. Everclear
2 oz. Vodka   2 oz. Triple Sec
4 oz. Orange Juice   4 oz. Pineapple Juice
1/2 cup cracked Ice

Mix in shaker. Strain into a chilled highball glass.

Atlantic Dolphin S**t

1 oz. Kahlua   1 oz. Heavy Cream
1 oz. Dark Rum   1 oz. Crème de Cacao
2 crushed Oreo Cookies   2 oz. Milk

Put into a highball glass.

Aztec

1 1/2 oz. Tequila   1 oz. Kahlua
1 oz. White Crème de Cacao
1 1/2 dashes Curaçao

Shake with cracked ice and strain.

B-52

Equal Parts: Kahlua, Bailey's, Grand Marnier

Layer in exact order in a shot glass.

Baby, Baby, Baby

1 oz. Stolichnaya   3/4 oz. Grand Marnier
1/2 oz. Bailey's

Hand swirl over ice. Strain into a chilled cocktail glass.

Baby's Bottom

[2]

1 1/2 oz. Whiskey
1/2 oz. White Crème de Cacao
1/2 oz. White Crème de Menthe

Stir over ice. Strain into chilled cocktail glass.

Bacardi Cocktail

[2]

1 1/4 oz. Bacardi Rum   splash of Sour Mix
dash of Grenadine

Shake with ice. Serve in a chilled cocktail glass.
Garnish with lime wedge.

Back Street Banger

[8]

1/2 oz. Bourbon   1/2 oz. Bailey's

Serve on the rocks.

Bad Habit

[8]

1/2 oz. Vodka   1/2 oz. Peach Schnapps

Serve over ice.

Bahama Breeze

[10]

1 oz. Dark Rum   1/2 oz. Banana Liqueur
1/2 oz. Apricot Liqueur 1/2 oz. Coconut Rum
1/4 oz. Grenadine   1/4 oz. Honey
1/2 oz. Lemon Juice   1 oz. Orange Juice
1 oz. Pineapple Juice

Blend well with ice cubes. Garnish with orange
wedge.

Bahama Mama

[18]

1 1/2 oz. Coconut Rum 1/2 oz. Triple Sec
Orange Juice   Pineapple Juice
dash Grenadine
splash of Cream of Coconut

Shake over ice. Serve in a hurricane glass.
Garnish with an orange slice and cherry.

Bahama Nut

[3]

1 oz. Nassau Royale   1 oz. Frangelico

Layer in exact order.

Bahamian Rapture

[3]

1 oz. Dark Rum   1/2 oz. Cream
1/4 oz. Coconut Rum Liqueur
1/4 oz. Crème de Banana

Mix Dark Rum and cream. Pour into glass.
Layer remaining in exact order (Crème de
Banana, Coconut Rum Liqueur).

Bahamian Special

[8]

1 oz. Myers's Dark Rum
1 oz. Cream of Coconut

Combine with ice and stir.

Bailey's Comet

[3]

3/4 oz. Bailey's   1/2 oz. Vodka
1 splash Club Soda   1 splash Cream
1/2 oz. Dark Crème de Cacao

Combine with ice and shake. Strain and serve
straight up.

Bailey's Mint Kiss

[4]

3/4 oz. Bailey's   3/4 oz. Kahlua
3/4 oz. Rumple Minze   Coffee as needed
dash Whipped Cream

Combine liqueurs and stir. Fill with coffee and
top with whipped cream.

Banana Banshee Frozen

[10]

1 1/2 oz. Banana Liqueur
1 1/2 oz. White Crème de Cacao
1 1/2 oz. Cream

In blender mix at slow speed until smooth with
1/2 cup of cracked ice.

Banana Barbados

3/4 oz. Mount Gay Eclipse Rum
3/4 oz. Myers's Jamaican Rum
1/2 oz. Crème de Banana
splash of Sour mix
2 scoops Vanilla Ice Cream

Blend. Float a dash of Myers's. Serve in hurricane glass.

Banana Boat

Equal parts: Tia Maria, Kahlua, Peppermint Schnapps, Myers's Rum Cream

Layer in exact order into a shot glass.

Banana Daiquiri

1 oz. Rum   3/4 oz. Crème de Banana
splash of Sour Mix   dash of Simple Syrup
1 Banana

Blend until smooth. Serve in hurricane glass.

Banana Frost

1 oz. Amaretto   1 oz. Cream
1 Banana   2 oz. Ice
2 scoops Vanilla Ice Cream

Combine with crushed ice and blend until smooth. Garnish with a slice of banana.

Banana Java

1/2 oz. Banana Liqueur   1 oz. Coffee Liqueur
1/2 Banana   1 wedge Orange
4 oz. Ice

Combine with crushed ice and blend until smooth. Garnish with fruit.

Banana Margarita

2 oz. Tequila   1/2 oz. Crème de Banana
2 oz. Sour Mix   1/2 Banana
1 1/2 cups Ice

Combine with crushed ice until smooth. Pour into sugar rimmed glass. Garnish with lime.

Banana Punch

2 oz. Vodka   1/2 Lime
splash Club Soda   3 slices Banana
1 sprig Mint
1 1/2 tsp. Apricot Brandy

Combine all except club soda and stir. Add ice and club soda. Garnish with banana and mint.

Banana Rum Punch

1 oz. Rum   1/2 oz. Crème de Banana
splash of Orange Juice

Blend with ice. Serve in rocks glass.

Banana Smash Blend

1 Banana   2 oz. Coconut Syrup
1 oz. Orgeat Syrup 3 oz. Cream
3 oz. Ice

Combine with crushed ice until smooth. Garnish with whipped cream, banana and a cherry.

Banana Tree

1 oz. Banana Liqueur   1/2 oz. Galliano
1/2 oz. White Crème de Cacao
1/2 oz. Banana
5 oz. Vanilla Ice Cream
4 drops Vanilla Extract

Blend all with 1/4 cup ice until smooth. Garnish with banana slices.

Bananarama

3

3/4 oz. Kahlua   3/4 oz. Amaretto
3/4 oz. Crème de Banana
1/4 oz. Cream

Layer liqueurs in exact order. Float cream on top.

Banshee

6

1 oz. Crème De Banana   1/2 oz. Crème de Cacao
splash of Cream

Blend with ice. Strain into a flute glass.

Batido de Piña

1

2 1/2 oz. White Rum   5 oz. Pineapple
1 tsp. Powdered Sugar   4 oz. Ice

Combine with crushed ice and blend until smooth.

Bay Breeze

10

1 oz. Vodka   splash Pineapple Juice
splash Cranberry Juice

Serve over ice in a highball glass.

Bayberry Punch

13

2 quarts Brandy   8 oz. Curaçao
12 Lemons   10 oz. Powdered Sugar
16 oz. Tea   6 Oranges
6 oz. Grenadine

Slice fruit and combine all and mix. Add ice chunks before serving.

Beach Blanket Bingo

21

Equal parts: Cranberry Juice, Grapefruit Juice
splash of Soda

Stir juices over ice in a collins glass. Top with soda. Garnish with Lime wedge.

Beach Warmer

4

3/4 oz. Chambord   3/4 oz. Kahlua
Hot Chocolate

Stir in an Irish coffee mug.

Beachcomber

2

1 1/2 oz. Rum   1/2 oz. Triple Sec
1/2 oz. Lime Juice

Shake with ice. Pour into a chilled cocktail glass.

Beam Me Up Scotty

3

3/4 oz. Kahlua   3/4 oz. Crème de Banana
3/4 oz. Bailey's

Layer in exact order.

Beautiful Thing

3

3/4 oz. Bailey's   3/4 oz. Rumple Minze

Combine with ice and shake. Strain and serve straight up.

Bee Stinger

2

1 1/2 oz. Blackberry Brandy
1/2 oz. White Crème de Menthe

Shake with ice. Pour into a chilled cocktail glass.

Bee's Kiss

1 1/2 oz. White Rum   1 tsp. Honey
1 tsp. Heavy Cream

Combine with ice and shake. Strain and add ice.

Benedict

1 1/2 oz. Benedictine   1 1/2 oz. Scotch
fill Ginger Ale

Combine with ice and stir.

Bermuda Bouquet

1 oz. Apricot Brandy   1/2 tsp. Curaçao
1 1/2 oz. Dry Gin   1/2 tsp. Grenadine
1 tsp. Powdered Sugar   1 twist Orange

Combine with ice and shake. Strain and add ice.
Garnish with fruit.

Bermuda Highball

3/4 oz. Gin   3/4 oz. Brandy
3/4 oz. Dry Vermouth   splash of Ginger Ale

Build in a highball glass. Garnish with lemon twist.

Bermuda Rose Cocktail

1 1/2 oz. Gin   1 dash Apricot Brandy
1 dash Grenadine

Shake and strain.

Berry Melon

1/4 oz. Midori   1/4 oz. Orange Juice
1/2 oz. Blueberry Schnapps

Combine with ice and stir. Strain and serve straight up.

Between the Sheets

1 oz. Brandy   1 oz. Triple Sec
1 oz. Light Rum

Shake and strain.

Big Fat One

1/2 oz. Cointreau   1/2 oz. Midori
1/2 oz. Vodka   1 slice Orange

Combine, add ice and shake. Strain and serve straight up.

Bikini

3/4 oz. Grand Marnier   3/4 oz. Vodka
3/4 oz. Strawberry Schnapps

Layer liqueurs in exact order.

Bikini Line ③

1/2 oz. Chambord	1/2 oz. Tia Maria
1/2 oz. Vodka	1 splash Pineapple Juice

Combine with ice and shake. Strain and serve straight up.

Bikini Line-2 ③

1/2 oz. Chambord	1/2 oz. Tia Maria
1/2 oz. Vodka	

Layer in shot glass.

Bird of Paradise ⑩

2 oz. Gin	splash Club Soda
1 Egg White	1 tsp. Grenadine
2 Tbsp. Lemon Juice	1 tsp. Powdered Sugar

Combine all but soda with ice and shake. Strain and add ice.

Bishop's Cocktail ②

1 1/2 oz. Gin	1 1/2 oz. Ginger Wine

Combine with ice and shake. Strain and serve straight up.

Bitch's Itch ㉑

1 1/2 oz. Light Rum	1/2 oz. Triple Sec
1 tsp. 151 Rum	1 oz. Lime Juice
1/2 oz. Sugar Syrup	1 pinch Cinnamon
1 pinch Nutmeg	
1/2 oz. White Crème de Cacao	

Combine all but 151 Rum with ice and shake. Strain and add ice. Float 151 Rum and sprinkle cinnamon and nutmeg.

Bit-O-Honey ③

3/4 oz. Apple Schnapps   3/4 oz. Frangelico

Hand swirl with ice. Strain into shot glass.

Bitter Lemon Cooler ②

1 1/2 oz. Dry Gin	1 1/2 oz. Dry Vermouth
1 tsp. Lemon Juice	dash Lemon-Lime Soda
1 tsp. Raspberry Syrup	1 twist Lemon

Combine all but soda with ice and shake. Strain and add soda and ice. Garnish with lemon.

Black Eye ⑪

1 1/2 oz. Vodka	1 twist Lime
2 Tbsp. Lime Juice	
2 tsp. Blackberry Brandy	

Combine with ice and shake. Strain and serve straight up. Garnish with lime twist.

Black Forest Martini ⑯

Equal Parts: Absolut Citron, Frangelico
splash Maraschino Cherry Juice

Shake and strain into a martini glass. Garnish with a maraschino cherry.

Black Jack ④

1 oz. Jack Daniel's   1 oz. Rumple Minze
dash Coffee

Combine liqueurs and stir. Fill with coffee.

Black Jamaican ⑧

1 1/2 oz. Myers's Dark Rum
1/2 oz. Tia Maria

Combine with ice and stir.

Black Magic
8

3/4 oz. Kahlua   1 1/2 oz. Vodka
1 dash Lemon Juice

Combine with ice and shake. Strain and add ice.

Black Maria
11

2 oz. Coffee Brandy   2 oz. White Rum
4 oz. Coffee   2 tsp. Powdered Sugar

Combine with ice and stir.

Black Orchid
8

1 oz. Bacardi Black   1 oz. Chambord
1/2 oz. Grenadine   1/2 oz. Grenadine
1/2 oz. 7-Up

Shake with ice. Strain into rocks glass. Top with 7-Up.

Black Russian
8

1 1/2 oz. Vodka   3/4 oz. Kahlua

Pour over ice in a rocks glass.

Black Sand
3

1/2 oz. Kahlua   1/2 oz. Black Sambuca
1/2 oz. Amaretto

Layer in exact order into a shot glass.

Black Widow
8

1 oz. Jagermeister   1 oz. Sambuca

Combine with ice and stir.

Blackberry Fizz
21

3 oz. Orange Juice   3 oz. Sour Mix
1 slice Orange
1/4 oz. Lemon-Lime Soda
1 oz. Blackberry Brandy

Combine with ice and stir.

Blackberry Flip
19

1 splash Cream   2 oz. Blackberry Brandy
1 Egg   1/2 splash Sugar Syrup
1 dash Nutmeg

Combine with ice and shake. Strain and serve straight up.

Blackjack
19

1 1/2 oz. Kirsch   1 dash Brandy
1 1/2 oz. Coffee

Combine iced coffee with Kirsch and crushed ice. Top with Brandy and stir.

Black-out Shooter
8

1/2 oz. Gin
1/2 oz. Blackberry Brandy
1 splash Lime Juice

Combine with ice and shake. Strain and serve straight up.

Blarney Stone Sour
8

1 1/2 oz. Irish Whiskey   splash of Orange Juice
splash of Sour Mix

Blend over ice. Garnish with orange slice and cherry.

Blast From The Past

1/2 oz. Grand Marnier   1/2 oz. Jose Cuervo Gold
1/2 oz. Tia Maria   dash Espresso
dash Whipped Cream

Combine liqueurs and stir. Fill with espresso and top with whipped cream.

Blended Frog

1 oz. Vodka   3 oz. Cranberry Juice
3 oz. Ice

Combine with crushed ice and blend until smooth.

Blood and Sand

1 oz. Cherry Brandy   1 oz. Scotch
1 oz. Sweet Vermouth   1 oz. Orange Juice

Combine with ice and shake. Strain and add ice.

Blood Clot Shooter

1/2 oz. 151 Rum   1 dash Grenadine
1 dash Cream

Combine ingredients and float cream.

Blood Hound

(frozen)

1 1/2 oz. Gin   1/2 oz. Dry Vermouth
3 oz. Ice
1/2 oz. Sweet Vermouth
1 tsp. Strawberry Schnapps

Combine with crushed ice and blend until smooth.

Blood Hound-2

1 oz. Dry Sack Sherry   1 oz. Vodka
dash Bloody Mary Mix   1 slice Lime
1 stick Celery

Combine with ice and stir. Strain and garnish with lime and celery.

Bloody Bull

1 oz. Vodka   2 1/2 oz. Bull Shot
1 slice Lime   1 stick Celery

Combine with ice and stir. Garnish with lime and cherry.

Bloody Job

Equal parts: Kahlua, Bailey's, Vodka

Layer in shot glass. Top with whipped cream.

Bloody Maria

1 1/2 oz. Tequila   dash of Worcestershire
dash of Tabasco   dash of Salt and Pepper
dash of Lime Juice   Tomato Juice to fill

Build in exact order in a tall glass. Garnish with a celery stalk, lime wedge.

Blue Bell

1 Tbsp. Dry Vermouth   1 1/2 oz. Whiskey
2 dashes Angostura Bitters

Combine with ice and shake. Strain and add ice.

Blue Devil

1/2 oz. Blue Curaçao   1 oz. Gin
1 1/2 oz. Sour Mix

Combine with ice and shake. Strain and serve straight up.

Blue Fox

1 oz. Blue Curaçao   1 oz. Southern Comfort

Layer liqueurs in exact order.

Blue Hawaii

1 oz. Blue Curaçao   1 oz. Rum
splash of Sour Mix   splash of Pineapple Juice

Shake. Pour over ice in tall glass.

Blue Lagoon

1 oz. Malibu Rum   1/2 oz. Blue Curaçao
1/2 oz. Pineapple Juice

Pour Rum & pineapple juice over ice in highball glass. Float Blue Curaçao.

Blue
Lagoon Margarita

1 1/4 oz. Cuervo Gold   3/4 oz. Blue Curaçao
Pineapple Juice to fill   Splash 7-UP
1 count Rose's Lime Juice

Shake. Pour over ice.

Blue Max

1 oz. Absolut   1/2 oz. Blue Curaçao
2 splashes Cream   1 slice Orange
3 splashes Pineapple Juice
2 splashes Cream of Coconut

Combine with ice and blend. Garnish with fruit.

Blue Mondays

1 oz. Tequila   1 oz. Cointreau
1 oz. Midori   1 oz. Lemon Juice
2 Kiwi Fruits peeled

Frost the rim of goblet with salt. Combine ingredients in blender with ice. Blend until smooth.

Blue Moon

3 dashes Crème Yvette   3/4 oz. Dry Vermouth
1 1/2 oz. Gin   2 dashes Orange Bitters

Combine with ice and shake. Strain and add ice.

Blue Moon Café

1/2 oz. Champagne   1/2 oz. Blue Curaçao
1/2 oz. Orange Juice

Combine with ice and shake. Strain and serve straight up.

Blue Mountain

3/4 oz. Tia Maria   3/4 oz. Vodka
1 1/2 oz. Orange Juice
1 1/2 oz. Jamaican Rum

Combine with ice and shake. Strain and add ice.

Blue Nuts

1/2 oz. Absolut   3/4 oz. Malibu
1/2 oz. Cranberry Juice
1/2 oz. Pineapple Juice
3/4 oz. Blueberry Schnapps

Combine with ice and shake. Strain and serve straight up.

Blue Popper

1 oz. Tequila   1/4 oz. Blue Curaçao

Layer into a shot glass.

Blue Shark

2 dashes Blue Curaçao   1 1/2 oz. Tequila
1 1/2 oz. Vodka

Combine with ice and shake. Strain and add ice.

Blue S**ts

1 oz. Blue Curaçao   1 oz. Vodka
1 oz. Pineapple Juice

Combine with ice and shake. Strain and serve straight up.

Blue Sky

1 1/4 oz. Blue Curaçao   fill with Milk

Build in a highball glass.

Blue Smoke

1 dash Blue Curaçao   1 1/2 oz. Tequila
4 oz. Orange Juice

Combine all but Blue Curaçao with ice and stir. Float Blue Curaçao on top.

Blue Whale

1/2 oz. Blue Curaçao   1 oz. Rum
splash Pineapple Juice

Shake with ice. Serve up in a chilled cocktail glass or on the rocks.

Blueberry Rum Fizz

1/2 oz. Triple Sec   2 1/2 oz. White Rum
1 Tbsp. Lemon Juice   1 tsp. Blueberry Syrup
5 Blueberries   splash Club Soda
1 slice Lemon

Combine all but soda with ice and shake. Strain and add soda and ice. Garnish with fruit.

Bluebird

1/2 oz. Curaçao   2 1/2 oz. Gin
1 Cherry   1 twist Lemon
3 dashes Angostura Bitters

Combine with ice and shake. Strain and add ice. Garnish with fruit.

Bluemoon

1 1/4 oz. Blue Curaçao   3/4 oz. Vodka
dash Cream

Layer in exact order, float cream.

Boat Cocktail

1/2 oz. Brandy   1 1/4 oz. Vodka
1 1/4 oz. Orange Juice

Combine vodka and orange juice with ice and shake. Strain and float brandy on top.

Boat Drink

1 oz. Brandy   1 oz. Vodka
1 oz. Orange Juice

Combine all but brandy with ice and shake. Strain and float brandy on top.

Bob Marley

Equal parts: Peppermint Schnapps, Myers's Rum

Layer into a shot glass.

Bobby Burns

1/2 oz. Drambuie   1 1/2 oz. Scotch
1/2 oz. Sweet Vermouth

Combine with ice and stir. Strain and serve straight up.

Bombay

1 oz. Brandy
1/2 oz. Dry Vermouth
1 oz. Sweet Vermouth
2 dashes Curaçao
1 dash Pernod

Combine with ice and shake. Strain and add ice.

 Bombay Punch

1 bottle Cognac
1 bottle Dry Sherry
4 bottles Champagne
8 oz. Lemon Juice
4 oz. Curaçao
4 oz. Maraschino
2 liters Club Soda
1 tsp. Sugar

Combine all but Champagne and soda. Before serving add Champagne, soda and ice chunks.

Bomber Punch

1 pint Sherry
1 1/2 oz. Orange Juice
1 1/2 oz. Cointreau
2 dashes Orange Bitters

Combine with ice and stir. Garnish with fruit.

Bomber Shooter

1/2 oz. Amaretto
2 splashes Pineapple Juice
1/2 oz. Absolut

Combine with ice and shake. Strain and serve straight up.

Bombino

1 1/4 oz. Vodka
splash of Cream
3/4 oz. Amaretto

Shake. Pour over ice in rocks glass.

 Bonaire Booty

3/4 oz. Amaretto
1/2 oz. Gold Rum
1 oz. Chocolate Schnapps
1 oz. Cream

Combine with ice and shake. Strain and serve straight up.

Border Conflict Shooter

1 oz. Stolichnaya
1 oz. Peppermint Schnapps
1 splash Grenadine

Combine with ice and stir. Strain and serve straight up.

Borinque

1 tsp. 151 Rum
1 Tbsp. Lime Juice
1/2 oz. Orange Juice
1 1/2 oz. White Rum
1 slice Orange
1/2 oz. Passion Fruit Juice

Combine with ice and shake. Strain over crushed ice. Garnish with fruit.

Bosom Caresser

1 1/2 oz. Brandy
1 Egg Yolk
1/2 oz. Triple Sec
2 dashes Grenadine

Combine with ice and shake. Strain and serve straight up.

Boston Cocktail

1 oz. Apricot Brandy
1 tsp. Grenadine
1 oz. Dry Gin
1 tsp. Lemon Juice

Combine with ice and shake. Strain and add ice.

Bottom Bouncer

1 oz. Bailey's
1 oz. Butterscotch Schnapps

Pour over ice in rocks glass & strain into shot glass.

Bourbon a la Crème

2 oz. Bourbon
1 oz. Dark Crème de Cacao
2 Vanilla beans

Combine with ice and chill for 1-2 hours. Shake and serve straight up.

Bourbon Branca

2 oz. Bourbon
1 twist Lemon
1 tsp. Fernet Branca

Combine with ice and stir. Garnish with fruit.

Bourbon Cardinal

1 1/2 oz. Bourbon
1 Tbsp. Cranberry Juice
2 tsp. Lemon Juice
2 Cherry
1 dash Cherry Juice
1 Tbsp. Grapefruit Juice
1 Tbsp. Sugar Syrup

Combine with ice and shake. Strain and serve straight up. Garnish with fruit.

Bourbon Collins

2 oz. Bourbon
1 slice Lemon
1 Tbsp. Sugar Syrup
2 dashes Peychaud's Bitters
splash Club Soda
1/2 oz. Lemon Juice

Combine all but soda with ice and shake well. Strain and add soda and ice. Garnish with fruit.

Bourbon Flip

2 oz. Wild Turkey
1 splash Cream
1 dash Nutmeg
1/2 splash Sugar Syrup
1 Egg

Combine with ice and shake. Strain and serve straight up.

Bourbon Punch

1 quart Bourbon
4 oz. Grenadine
3 slices Orange
3 oz. Sugar
1 quart Club Soda
3 slices Lemon
6 oz. Orange Juice
3 oz. Lemon Juice

Combine with ice and stir.

Bourbon Sour

2 oz. Bourbon
2 tsp. Sugar Syrup
2 Tbsp. Lemon Juice
1 slice Orange

Combine with ice and shake. Strain and serve straight up. Garnish with fruit.

Bourbonville

1 1/2 oz. Bourbon
1 1/2 tsp. Lime Juice
splash Club Soda
1 twist Lime

Combine all but soda with ice and shake. Strain and add soda and ice. Garnish with fruit.

Brahma Bull

1 1/2 oz. Jose Cuervo Gold   1/2 oz. Tia Maria

Combine with ice and stir.

Brain Eraser

1 oz. Vodka
1/2 oz. Amaretto
1/2 oz. Kahlua
1 splash Club Soda

Combine.

Brain Fade

1 1/2 oz. Applejack
1/2 oz. Lime Juice
1/2 oz. Crème de Banana
1/2 oz. Orange Juice

Mix in blender until slushy.

Brandied Banana Collins

1 1/2 oz. Brandy
splash Club Soda
2 tsp. Lemon Juice
1 oz. Banana Liqueur
1 slice Lemon

Combine all but soda with ice and shake. Strain and add soda and ice. Garnish with fruit.

Brandied Boat

1 oz. Brandy
1 oz. Port
1 slice Orange
1 tsp. Maraschino
2 tsp. Lemon Juice

Combine with ice and shake. Strain and add ice. Garnish with fruit.

Brandied Mocha Punch

10 oz. Brandy
1 quart Coffee
dash Whipped Cream
1 dash Cinnamon
1 quart Hot Chocolate
6 chips Chocolate

Combine coffee, hot chocolate and Brandy. Garnish with whipped cream, chocolate chips and cinnamon. Serve hot.

Brandy Alexander

1 oz. Dark Crème de Cacao
Cream
1 oz. Brandy

Blend with ice. Strain into flute glass. Garnish with a sprinkle of nutmeg.

Brandy Berry Fix

2 oz. Brandy
2 tsp. Lemon Juice
1 tsp. Strawberry Liqueur
1 tsp. Sugar Syrup

Combine with ice and shake. Strain over crushed ice.

Brandy Boat

2 oz. Brandy
1/2 oz. Club Soda
1 tsp. Lemon Juice
1 tsp. Pineapple Juice
1 dash Lime Juice
1 dash Rum
1 slice Lemon
1 slice Orange
2 tsp. Sugar Syrup

Combine all but Rum, and soda with ice and shake. Strain and add soda and crushed ice. Float Rum on top. Garnish with fruit.

Brandy Chiller

1 1/2 oz. Brandy
3 oz. Ginger Ale

Combine with ice and stir.

Brandy Fix

1 1/2 oz. Brandy
1 tsp. Lime Juice
1 oz. Cherry Brandy
1 tsp. Sugar Syrup

Combine with ice and shake. Strain over crushed ice.

Brandy Fizz

1 1/4 oz. Brandy
dash of Soda
splash of Sour Mix

Shake Brandy & Sour Mix over ice. Pour in a tall glass. Add soda to fill. Garnish with an orange slice.

Brandy Hot Toddy

2 1/2 oz. Brandy
1 dash Nutmeg
1 twist Lemon
1/2 tsp. Sugar

Combine with hot water and stir. Garnish with fruit and nutmeg.

Brandy Manhattan

1 1/2 oz. Brandy   1/2 oz. Sweet Vermouth
1 Cherry

Combine with ice and stir. Strain and serve straight up. Garnish with cherry.

———————————————

Brandy Sour

2 oz. Brandy   2 tsp. Lemon Juice
1 tsp. Orange Juice   1 tsp. Sugar Syrup
1 slice Lemon

Combine with ice and shake. Strain and serve straight up. Garnish with fruit.

———————————————

Brandy Stinger

1 1/2 oz. Brandy   1 twist Lemon
1 Tbsp. White Crème de Menthe

Combine with ice and shake. Strain and add ice. Garnish with fruit.

Brave Bull

1 1/4 oz. Tequila   3/4 oz. Kahlua

Build over ice in a rocks glass. Garnish with a lemon twist.

———————————————

Brittany

1 1/2 oz. Gin   2 tsp. Amer Picon
1 tsp. Lemon Juice   1 twist Orange
1 tsp. Orange Juice

Combine with ice and shake. Strain and add ice. Garnish with fruit.

———————————————

Brown Nipple Shooter

1 oz. Kahlua   1 oz. Bailey's
1 dash Grenadine

Combine with ice and stir. Pour grenadine in center.

Bruise

2 oz. Absolut Mandrin   splash 7 UP
1/2 oz. Blue Curaçao
Pineapple Juice to fill
1/2 oz. Razzmatazz Schnapps

Build in highball glass.

Bubble Gum

1/2 oz. Midori   1/2 oz. Crème de Banana
1/2 oz. Vodka   1/4 oz. Grenadine
1/2 oz. Orange Juice   1/2 oz. Sour Mix

Combine with ice and shake. Strain and serve
straight up.

Buckaroo Banzai

1 1/2 oz. Wild Turkey   1/2 oz. Plum Wine

Layer in exact order.

Bull Shoot

1/2 oz. Kahlua   1/2 oz. Rum
1/2 oz. Tequila

Layer liqueurs in exact order.

Bull Witch Project

1 oz. Black Vodka   1 oz. Malibu
splash Cranberry Juice   splash Pineapple Juice
splash Red Bull

Shake all ingredients and strain into a martini
glass. Garnish with cinnamon sticks arranged
like the Blair Witch Trees.

Bull's Milk

1 1/2 oz. Brandy   1 oz. Rum
8 oz. Milk   1 tsp. Powdered Sugar
1 dash Nutmeg   1 dash Cinnamon

Combine with ice and shake. Strain and add ice.
Dust with cinnamon and nutmeg.

Bullshot

1 1/2 oz. Vodka   1 dash Worcestershire
4 oz. Beef Bouillon

Combine with ice and stir. Garnish with fruit.

Bumble Bee

1 oz. Southern Comfort   1 oz. Jack Daniel's
as needed Water

Combine liqueurs with ice and stir. Water used
on the side.

Bungee Jumper

1/4 oz. Amaretto   1 1/4 oz. Irish Mist
1/2 oz. Cream   4 oz. Orange Juice

Combine all but Amaretto with ice and shake.
Strain and add ice. Float Amaretto on top.

Bunny Hug

1 oz. Gin   1 1/2 Tbsp. Pernod
1 oz. Whiskey

Combine with ice and shake. Strain and add ice.

Bushwacker

1 1/2 oz. 151 Rum   1 oz. Amaretto
2 oz. Kahlua   1 oz. Crème de Cacao
1 oz. Bailey's   1 oz. Vodka
2 oz. Pineapple Juice   4 oz. Coconut Cream

Mix in blender with crushed ice. Blend until smooth.

Bust A Nut

1 oz. Beer   1/3 oz. Amaretto
1/3 oz. Galliano   1/3 oz. Rum
1/3 oz. Gin   1/3 oz. Triple Sec
1/3 oz. Vodka

Combine with ice and shake. Strain and serve straight up.

Busted Cherry

Equal parts: Kahlua, Half & Half, Cherry Brandy

Layer in exact order in shot glass.

Buttery Nipple

1 oz. Butterscotch Schnapps   1 oz. Bailey's

Layer in shot glass.

By The Pool

3/4 oz. Midori   3/4 oz. Peach Schnapps
3/4 oz. Lemon-Lime   Soda
3/4 oz. Orange Juice

Combine with ice and shake. Strain and serve straight up.

Café Cocktail

1 oz. Cognac   1 1/2 tsp. Sugar Syrup
1 twist Lemon   2 oz. Coffee
1 oz. Dark Crème de Cacao

Combine with ice and shake well. Strain and add ice. Garnish with fruit.

Café Di Amaretto

1 oz. Amaretto   to fill Coffee
dash Whipped Cream

Combine and stir gently. Top with whipped cream.

Café Grog

1 oz. Brandy   2 oz. Jamaican Rum
4 oz. Coffee   1 tsp. Sugar
1 twist Lemon

Combine liqueurs with hot coffee and stir. Add sugar as needed. Garnish with lemon twist.

California Lemonade

2 oz. Whiskey   1 dash Grenadine
2 oz. Sour Mix

Shake and strain.

California Screw

1 oz. Vodka   1 1/2 oz. Grapefruit Juice
1 1/2 oz. Orange Juice

Combine with ice and stir.

Calypso Cooler
2

dash of Grenadine   *splash Orange Juice*
3/4 oz. Peach Schnapps
1 1/4 oz. Captain Morgan Spiced Rum

Shake well.

_____

Calypso Daiquiri
14

2 1/2 oz. Sour Mix   *1 Banana*
1/2 oz. Half & Half
1 tsp. Vanilla Extract
1 1/4 oz. Myers's Jamaican Rum

Blend with ice.

_____

Canadian Cherry
21

1 tsp. Lemon Juice   *1 tsp. Orange Juice*
1 1/2 oz. Canadian Whiskey
1/2 oz. Peter Heering

Sugar frost glass rim with Peter Heering.
Combine with ice and shake. Strain and add ice.

_____

Candy Ass
3

1/2 oz. Chambord   *1/2 oz. Mozart*

Combine with ice and stir. Strain and serve straight up.

_____

Capri
8

1 1/2 oz. Crème de Banana
1 1/2 oz. White Crème de Cacao
1 1/2 oz. Cream

Shake over ice.

Captain Cook
10

1 oz. Light Rum   *1/4 oz. Grand Marnier*
splash Pineapple Juice   *1 Cherry*

Combine with ice and stir.

_____

Captain Morgan Cooler
18

1 oz. Captain Morgan   *2 oz. Pineapple Juice*
splash Cherry Juice   *dash of Grenadine*

Blend with ice.

_____

Captain's Blood
2

2 oz. Rum   *1 oz. Lime Juice*
2 dashes Bitters

Shake well with ice. Strain into cocktail glass.

_____

Captain's Cooler
21

1 oz. Captain Morgan   *1/2 oz. Grand Marnier*
1/2 oz. Triple Sec   *splash Lemon-Lime Soda*
1/2 oz. Cranberry Juice   *1 oz. Orange Juice*
1/2 oz. Rose's Lime Juice

Combine all but soda and shake. Strain and add ice. Fill with soda.

_____

Car Crash
8

1 oz. Southern Comfort   *1 oz. Triple Sec*
1 oz. Crème de Noyaux   *splash Lemon-Lime Soda*
splash Sour Mix

Combine with ice and stir.

Cardinal

2

3/4 oz. Dry Vermouth   1 Tbsp. Orange Juice
1 Tbsp. Tomato Juice   1 Olive

Combine with ice and shake. Strain and serve
straight up.

_____

Cardinal Cocktail

8

2 oz. White Rum   1 tsp. Triple Sec
1 1/2 Tbsp. Lime Juice   1 tsp. Almond Extract
1 tsp. Grenadine   a slice of Lime

Combine with ice and shake. Strain and add ice.
Garnish with fruit.

_____

Cardinal Punch

13

16 oz. Brandy   64 oz. Claret
1 split Champagne   8 oz. Sweet Vermouth
16 oz. White Rum   32 oz. Club Soda
dash Powdered Sugar

Combine with ice and stir. Garnish with fruits.

_____

Cardinal Sin Punch

13

1 bottle Champagne   1 pint Jamaican Rum
8 oz. Sweet Vermouth   2 quarts Claret
1 quart Club Soda   6 oz. Powdered Sugar
3 cups Lemon Juice   6 slices Orange
6 slices Lemon

Combine all but champagne and soda with ice
and stir. Add ice chunks, club soda and champagne.

_____

Carib Cocktail

8

1 1/2 oz. White Rum   1 oz. Lime Juice
1 oz. Pineapple Juice

Combine with ice and shake. Strain and add ice.

Caribbean

6

1 quart Beer   10 Tbsp. Crème de Banana
1 Orange   1 Kiwi

Slice fruit and cover with crème. Chill for several
hours. Put several fruit slices and liqueur in glass
and fill with beer.

_____

Caribbean Berry

3

1/4 oz. Coconut Rum   dash Midori
dash Peach Schnapps   dash Cranberry Juice
1/2 oz. Myers's Jamaican Rum

Shake over ice. Strain into shot glass.

_____

Caribbean Breeze

21

2 oz. Coconut Rum   1 oz. Vodka
splash Orange Juice   dash Grenadine

Serve in collins glass over ice.

_____

Caribbean Champagne

19

4 oz. Champagne   1/2 tsp. White Rum
1 slice Banana   1/2 tsp. Banana Liqueur
2 dashes Orange Bittters

Combine and stir. Garnish with fruit.

_____

Caribbean Cocktail

10

2 1/2 oz. White Rum   Club Soda to fill
2 Tbsp. Lime Juice   2 dashes Orange Bitters
8 oz. Pineapple Juice   1 oz. Sugar Syrup

Combine all but soda with ice and shake. Strain
and add soda and ice.

Caribbean Coffee

④

1 oz. Dark Rum   3/4 oz. Tia Maria
Coffee   Whipped Cream

Combine Liqueurs. Add coffee in mug. Top with whipped cream.

Caribbean Cruise

⑱

1 oz. Dark Rum   3/4 oz. Tia Maria
splash Orange Juice   splash Pineapple Juice
3/4 oz. Cream of Coconut
1 oz. Myers's Jamaican Rum

Blend with ice. Garnish with a lemon twist.

Caribbean Dream

④

Coffee to fill   1/2 oz. Crème de Banana
1/2 oz. Myers's Dark Rum
1/2 oz. White Crème de Cacao
dash Whipped Cream

Combine liqueurs and stir. Fill with coffee. Top with whipped cream.

Caribbean Hurricane

㉑

1 1/2 oz. White Rum   1/2 oz. Rose's Lime Juice
1/2 oz. Grenadine   2 oz. Orange Juice
2 oz. Pineapple Juice
2 dashes Sugar Syrup
1 1/2 oz. Myers's Dark Rum

Combine with ice and shake. Strain and add ice.

Caribbean Joy

⑩

2 dashes Cointreau   1 1/2 oz. Scotch
2 tsp. Lime Juice   1 tsp. Powdered Sugar

Combine with ice and shake. Strain and add ice.

Caribbean Sea

⑱

1/2 oz. Blue Curaçao   1 1/2 oz. Jamaican Rum
3 oz. Pineapple Juice   1 1/2 oz. Coconut Cream

Mix in blender with 1/2 cup ice. Blend until smooth.

Caribbean Sunset

③

1/2 oz. Chambord   1 splash Coffee
1/2 oz. Tia Maria   Cream
1/2 oz. Myers's Rum

Layer liqueurs in exact order. Top with coffee.

Cartel Buster

③

3/4 oz. Tia Maria   3/4 oz. Grand Marnier
3/4 oz. Jose Cuervo Gold

Layer liqueurs in exact order.

Cartel Shooter

③

3/4 oz. Chambord   3/4 oz. Vodka
1/2 oz. Sour Mix   1/4 oz. Grapefruit Juice

Combine with ice and shake. Strain and serve straight up.

Caruso

②

1 1/2 oz. Gin   1 oz. Dry Vermouth
splash of Green Crème de Menthe

Serve over ice. Strain into a chilled cocktail glass.

Casablanca

1 dash Curaçao   2 oz. Jamaican Rum
1 dash Maraschino   1tsp. Lime Juice
3 dashes Angostura Bitters

Combine with ice and shake. Strain and add ice.

_____

Casino

2 oz. Gin   1/2 tsp. Maraschino
1 dash Lemon Juice   2 dashes Orange Bitters

Combine with ice and shake. Strain and add ice.

_____

Cassis Punch

6 bottles White Wine   2 oz. Crème de Cassis
1 cup Strawberries

Combine crème and fruit and steep for 1-2 hours. Add wine and ice chunks.

_____

Cement Mixer

1 1/2 oz. Bailey's   1 oz. Rose's Lime Juice

Pour ingredients into separate glasses. Take Bailey's and swish around your mouth for fifteen seconds. Without swallowing, add lime juice and continue to swish around mouth. When mixture is complete swallow.

_____

Chambord Adrenalin

Equal parts of Chambord, Absolut

Shake Over ice. Strain into a shot glass.

Chambord Martini

1 oz. Absolut   1 oz. Chambord

Combine with ice and stir. Strain and serve straight up.

_____

Chambord Sour

1 oz. Chambord   1/2 splash Orange Juice
3 oz. Sour Mix

Combine with ice and shake. Strain and add ice.

_____

Champ Elysees Cocktail

1/2 oz. Benedictine   1 oz. Brandy
1 1/2 oz. Sour Mix
2 dashes Angostura Bitters

Combine with ice and shake. Strain and serve straight up.

_____

Champagne Cassis

6 oz. Champagne   1 dash Crème de Casis

Combine and stir.

_____

Champagne Cooler

1 oz. Brandy   1 oz. Triple Sec
Champagne to fill

Pour Brandy and Triple Sec half filled with cracked ice. Fill with chilled champagne. Stir gently.

9 Champagne Polonaise

3 dashes Cognac Champagne to fill
1/4 tsp. Blackberry Liqueur
1 tsp. Blackberry Brandy

Sugar frost glass with blackberry liqueur. Add Brandy and Cognac and stir. Fill with champagne.

---

6 Champagne Royale

Champagne to fill splash Chambord

Fill glass with champagne. Add splash of Chambord.

---

8 Chapala

1 1/2 oz. Tequila 2 tsp. Grenadine
2 tsp. Lemon Juice 2 tsp. Orange Juice
1 slice Orange

Combine with ice and shake. Strain and add ice. Garnish with fruit.

---

2 Chapel Hill

1 1/2 oz. Bourbon 1/2 oz. Triple Sec
1 Tbsp. Lemon Juice 1 twist Orange

Combine with ice and shake. Strain and serve straight up. Garnish with fruit.

---

10 Charlie Caplin

1 1/2 oz. Tanqueray 2 oz. Sweet & Sour Mix
1 oz. Grenadine

Shake and serve.

---

12 Chazzs Brainf**k

2 oz. Absolut Vodka 1 cup Quenched Lemons
2 oz. White Rum 1 cup Sprite
1 scoop crushed Ice

Put rum, vodka, ice and lemons in a shaker. Shake and add Sprite. Serve in a beer mug with a wide straw.

---

2 Cherry Bang!

1/2 oz. Cherry Marnier 1 1/2 oz. Gin
3 dashes Kirsch 1/4 oz. Maraschino
1/2 oz. Lemon Juice 1 Maraschino Cherry

Combine all but Kirsch with ice and shake. Strain and float Kirsch on top. Garnish with fruit.

---

3 Cherry Blossom Shooter

3/4 oz. Bailey's 3/4 oz. Kahlua
3/4 oz. Grenadine 1 Cherry

Place cherry at the bottom of the glass. Layer in exact order, Grenadine, Kahlua, Bailey's.

42

Cherry Bomb

1/2 oz. Kahlua   1/2 oz. Crème de Banana
1/2 oz. Myers's Rum Cream
1/2 oz. Cherry Schnapps

Layer liqueurs in exact order given.

Cherry Cheesecake

1/2 oz. Vanilla Schnapps
3/4 oz. Cranberry Juice

Pour over ice. Shake and strain.

Cherry Hooker

1 oz. Cherry Brandy   3 oz. Orange Juice
1 Lime Wheel

Combine with ice and stir.

Cherry Rum Fix

1 1/2 oz. Vodka   2 tsp. Peter Heering
2 tsp. Lemon Juice   2 tsp. Sugar Syrup
1 slice Lemon

Combine with ice and shake. Strain over crushed ice. Garnish with fruit.

Cherry Vodka

1 oz. Peter Heering   1 oz. Absolut
1 Lime Wheel
1 splash Rose's Lime Juice

Combine with ice and stir.

Chi Chi

1 oz. Vodka   Cream
Pineapple Juice
splash of Crème of Coconut

Blend with crushed ice. Serve in hurricane glass. Garnish with pineapple wedge.

Chihuahua

1 oz. Tequila   Lime Wheel
2 dashes Angostura Bitters
3 splashes Grapefruit Juice

Combine with ice and stir.

Chiquita

2 tsp. Banana Liqueur   1 1/2 oz. Vodka
2 tsp. Lime Juice   1 tsp. Sugar
2 oz. Banana   3 oz. Ice

Combine with crushed ice and blend until smooth.

Chocolate Almond Kiss

1/2 oz. Vodka   2 scoops of Ice Cream
1/2 oz. Frangelico
1/2 oz. Dark Crème de Cacao

Blend. Garnish with chocolate sprinkles.

Chocolate Black Russian

1 oz. Kahlua   1/2 oz. Vodka
2 scoops Chocolate Ice Cream

Mix in blender until smooth.

Chocolate Cake

1 1/4 oz. Stoli Vanil   3/4 oz. Frangelico

Shake and strain into small rocks glass. Garnish with sugar-coated lemon wedge.

Cinnamon Cola

1 1/2 oz. Cinnamon Schnapps Cola to fill

Pour schnapps and fill with ice. Add cola to fill.

Claret Punch

8 oz. Brandy   8 oz. Curaçao
3 quarts Claret   1 quart Club Soda
3 cups Lemon Juice   8 slices Orange
1 cup Powdered Sugar

Dissolve sugar in lemon juice. Add liqueurs and soda. Stir and add ice. Garnish with fruit.

Classic

1 oz. Brandy   1/2 oz. Maraschino
1/2 oz. Triple Sec   1 1/2 oz. Sour Mix
1 twist Lemon

Combine with ice and shake. Strain and serve straight up. Garnish with fruit.

Clover Club Royal

1 1/2 oz. Gin   1/2 Egg Yolk
1 tsp. Grenadine   1 Tbsp. Lemon Juice

Combine with ice and shake. Strain and add ice.

Club Martini

1 1/2 oz. Gin   2 tsp. Sweet Vermouth
1 Olive

Combine with ice and shake. Strain and serve straight up. Garnish with olive.

Coastal Kiss

1 oz. Amaretto   1 oz. Southern Comfort
6 oz. Pineapple Juice

Mix in blender with ice until smooth.

Cocaine

Equal parts of: Blackberry Brandy & Vodka, Splash of Grapefruit Juice

Shake with ice. Strain into chilled lowball glass.

Cocaine Lady

1/2 oz. Kahlua   1/2 oz. Absolut
1/2 oz. Light Rum   1/2 oz. Amaretto
3 oz. Cream   1/4 oz. Cola

Combine all but cola and shake. Add ice and top with cola.

Coco Colada

1 1/2 oz. Dark Crème de Cacao
4 oz. Pineapple Juice
1 1/2 oz. Cream of Coconut

Blend together with cracked ice until smooth and garnish with a pineapple spear.

Coco Loco

3/4 oz. Dark Rum   3/4 oz. Coconut Rum
1/2 oz. Orange Juice   1/2 oz. Pineapple Juice
1/4 oz. Grenadine   1/2 oz. Papaya Juice
1/2 oz. Cream of Coconut

Blend with ice until smooth.

Cocomotion

2 oz. Lime Juice   1 1/2 cup Ice
1 1/2 oz. Puerto Rican Dark Rum
4 oz. Coco Lopez Cream of Coconut

Blend with ice and serve in a margarita glass.

Coconut Colada

1 1/2 oz. Malibu
1 1/2 oz. Strawberry Colada Mix
3 oz. Orange Juice

Combine with ice and shake. Strain and serve straight up.

Coconut Daiquiri

1 oz. Rum   1 cup Ice
1 1/2 oz. Cream of Coconut
1/2 oz. Lime Juice

Combine with crushed ice and blend until smooth.

Coconut Gin

1 1/2 oz. Gin   1 tsp. Maraschino
2 tsp. Lemon Juice   1 tsp. Cream of Coconut

Combine with ice and shake. Strain and add ice.

Coconut Milk

1 oz. Rum   1 oz. Cream of Coconut
1 oz. Lemon-Lime Soda

Combine with ice and shake. Strain and serve straight up.

Coconut Punch

1 1/4 oz. Bacardi Light-Dry or Gold Rum
2 oz. Coco Lopez cream of Coconut
1/2 oz. Lemon Juice
3-4 Tbsp. Vanilla Ice Cream

Mix all ingredients in a shaker or blender with crushed ice and pour into a tall glass.

Coconut Tequila

1 1/2 oz. Tequila   1 tsp. Maraschino
4 oz. Ice   2 tsp. Cream of Coconut
2 tsp. Lemon Juice

Combine with crushed ice and blend until smooth. Strain and serve straight up.

Coconutsy

1 oz. Malibu   1/2 splash cream
3 splashes Pineapple Juice

Combine with ice and blend. Garnish with pineapple slice.

Coffee Alexander

2 oz. Coffee Brandy   2 oz. Light Cream
2 oz. White Crème de Cacao

Shake and strain.

Coffee Cocktail

4

1 1/2 oz. Apple Brandy   1 1/2 oz. Port
1 oz. Coffee   1 Egg Yolk
1 dash Nutmeg

Combine with ice and shake. Strain and add ice.
Top with nutmeg.

Coffee Flip

8

1 1/2 oz. Cognac   1 oz. Port
1 oz. Iced Coffee   1 Egg
1 1/2 tsp. Sugar Syrup   dash Nutmeg

Combine with ice and shake. Strain and serve
straight up. Top with nutmeg.

Coffee Grasshopper

3

3/4 oz. Coffee Liqueur
3/4 oz. White Crème de Menthe
3/4 oz. Heavy Cream

Combine with ice and shake. Strain and add ice.

Cointreau Cocktail

8

3/4 oz. Cointreau   3/4 oz. Gin
3/4 oz. Light Rum

Combine with ice and stir.

Collins

21

1 1/4 oz. Liquor*   Soda
1/2 Tbsp. Powdered Sugar
Juice of half a Lemon

Shake Liquor & lemon juice. Pour in collins
glass. Add splash soda. *Tom Collins—Gin •
Vodka Collins—Vodka • Rum Collins—Rum •
John Collins—Whiskey, usually Bourbon.

Colonial Tea Punch

13

1 1/2 oz. Brandy   1 quart Jamaican Rum
1 quart Dark Tea   12 Lemons
12 oz. Sugar

Combine lemon peels, lemon juice, tea, and sugar.
Steep for 1-2 hours. Add liquors and serve hot.

Colorado Mother F***er

2
8

Equal parts: Kahlua, Vodka, Gin, Rum, Tequila
& Cream
Splash of Cola

Shake with ice. Add splash of Cola. Serve up or
on the rocks.

Columbia

2

1 tsp. Kirsch   1/2 oz. Lemon Juice
1 1/2 oz. Light Rum
1/2 oz. Raspberry Schnapps

Combine with ice and shake. Strain and serve
straight up.

Columbia Skin

4

9 oz. Scotch   1 peel Lemon
6 slices Lemon   2 cups Water

Combine with boiling water and stir. Serve hot
and top with lemon slices.

Coma

3

3/4 oz. Kahlua   3/4 Anisette
3/4 oz. Grand Marnier

Layer in exact order.

Comet Cocktail

3/4 oz. Chambord   1 oz. Rum
3 scoops Vanilla Ice Cream
2 1/2 oz. Sour Mix
3/4 oz. Strawberry Schnapps

Combine and blend until smooth.

_____

Comfort Colada

2 oz. Pineapple Juice   1 or 2 cups crushed Ice
1 1/2 oz. Southern Comfort
1 oz. Cream of Coconut

Blend all ingredients until ice is completely broken up and liquid is frothy. Serve in tall glasses over ice. Garnish with cherries.

_____

Comfortable Freeze

1 oz. Southern Comfort
2 splashes Pineapple Juice
1 splash Grenadine

Combine with ice and blend.

_____

Comfortable Screw

1 oz. Vodka   3/4 oz. Southern Comfort
Orange Juice

Serve over ice in a highball glass.

_____

Conch Shell

4 oz. White Rum   2 tsp. Lime Juice

Combine with ice and shake. Strain and add ice.

Conchita

1 1/2 oz. Tequila   1 oz. Grapefruit Juice
1 dash Lemon Juice

Combine with ice and shake. Strain and add ice.

_____

Cointreau Orange Freeze

2 oz. Cointreau   4 oz. Orange Soda
Big scoop of Vanilla Ice Cream

Blend ingredients in blender. Pour into decorative glass and serve with an orange slice.

_____

Conquistador

1/2 oz. Bailey's   1/2 oz. Tia Maria
1/2 oz. Grand Marnier   1/2 oz. Jose Cuervo Gold

Layer liqueurs in exact order.

_____

Consuelo

1 shot Cointreau   1 shot Gold Rum
3 shots White Wine   dash Lime Juice

Stir. Add slices of citrus and ice.

_____

Cookie Crusher

2 scoops of Ice Cream   1 Oreo Cookie
1 oz. White Crème de Menthe
1 oz. Dark Crème de Cacao

Blend all. Top with Whipped Cream.

Copa De Oro

1 dash Maraschino   1 dash Pernod
1 1/2 oz. Gold Rum   3 tsp. Lime Juice
1 1/2 tsp. Sugar Syrup

Combine all but Pernod with 3 ounces crushed ice and blend. Strain and serve straight up. Top with Pernod.

Coral Reef

1 1/2 oz. Vodka
2 oz. Malibu or Coco Ribe
6 Strawberries or 1 Tbsp. Strawberry Preserves

Mix all ingredients with crushed ice . Pour into chilled wine goblet.

Corkscrew

1 1/2 oz. Rum & Dry Vermouth
1/2 oz. Peach Brandy

Serve over ice. Strain into chilled cocktail glass.

Cosmopolitan

1 oz. Cointreau   3 oz. Cranberry Juice
1 oz. Lemon Juice   1 1/2 oz. Vodka

Mix with ice in a shaker. Put into a cocktail glass and garnish with a slice of lime.

Cough Drop

Equal parts of: Blackberry Brandy & Peppermint Schnapps

Build in shot glass.

Count Curry

2 oz. Champagne   1/2 oz. Gin
1 tsp. Maple Syrup   1 sprig Mint

Combine and serve straight up. Garnish with mint.

Countdown

2 oz. Cointreau   1/2 Lime

Combine, add ice and shake. Strain and serve straight up.

Cranberry Cooler

Cranberry Juice   Splash of Soda

Combine in highball glass.

Creamsicle

1 1/2 oz. Galliano   1 1/2 oz. Grand Marnier
Splash of Cream   Splash of Orange Juice
Splash of Grenadine

Shake with ice & serve up in a champagne glass. Substitute ice cream for a frozen variation (omitting cream)

Creamy Screwdriver

2 oz. Vodka   1 Egg Yolk
4 oz. Orange Juice   1 tsp. Sugar Syrup
4 oz. Ice

Combine with crushed ice. Blend until smooth.

Creole Champagne Punch
13

1 bottle Champagne
8 oz. Curaçao
16 oz. Lemon Juice
8 slices Pineapple
2 cups Sugar

1 bottle White Wine
2 quarts Club Soda
1 cup Pineapple
16 Strawberries

Combine all but soda and stir. Add club soda. Garnish with crushed pineapple and fruits. Add ice

---

Cristiforo Columbo
21

1/2 oz. Campari
1 1/2 oz. Gin
1 dash Grenadine

1 dash Curaçao
Club Soda to fill
4 oz. Orange Juice

Combine all but club soda and Curaçao with ice. Shake, strain and add ice. Fill with soda and float Curaçao on top.

Crocodile
8

1/2 oz. Blue Curaçao
1 dash Orgeat Syrup
1/2 oz. Sour Mix

1/2 oz. Rum
1 oz. Orange Juice

Combine with ice and shake. Strain and add ice.

Crocodile Cooler
10

1 oz. Absolut Citron
splash of Sour Mix

1 oz. Midori
splash of Sprite

Shake all but Sprite. Pour into a tall glass. Top with Sprite.

C-Spot
12

1 1/4 oz. Peach Schnapps
2 oz. Cranberry Juice

Shake over ice. Strain into cocktail glass. Garnish with orange slice.

Cuba Libre
10

1 1/4 oz. Rum
dash of Lime Juice

1 1/4 oz. Coke

Serve over ice in highball glass. Garnish with lime wedge.

Cucaracha
2

One part Kahlua   Two parts Tequila

Mix in a cocktail glass. Light on fire for one minute and drink with a straw while burning.

Cuervo Acapulco Fizz
10

1 1/2 oz. Cuervo Gold
2 oz. Orange Juice
1 whole Egg
2 tsp. Granulated Sugar

1 1/2 oz. Cream
3 Ice Cubes
2 dashes Orange Bitters

Blend all ingredients together. Pour into a highball glass. Garnish with orange slice.

Cuervo Raspberry Margarita
15

1 1/2 oz. Cuervo Gold
1 oz. Triple Sec
1 oz. Major Peters' lime juice
1/2 cup Raspberries (frozen)
Fresh Raspberries for garnish

In blender combine 1/2 cup ice with ingredients. Blend until frothy.

Cum In A Cup

4 oz. Amaretto   2 tsp. Nestle Quik
2 scoops Vanilla Ice Cream
1 cup Milk

Make a thick milkshake and add Nestle Quik and
Amaretto. Serve in a parfait glass.

Curaçao Cooler

1 oz. Blue Curaçao   1 oz. Vodka
1 twist Lemon   2 tsp. Lemon Juice
2 tsp. Lime Juice   1 Lemon twist
Orange Juice to fill

Combine with ice and shake. Strain and add ice.
Garnish with fruit.

Dagger

Equal parts of: Tequila, Dark Crème de Cacao,
Peppermint Schnapps

Layer in shot glass.

Daiquiri

1 1/4 oz. Rum   Lime Juice
dash of Sour Mix

Shake with ice. Serve up in a flute glass.

Daisy Pusher

1/2 oz. Vodka   1/2 oz. Gin
1 shot of Bailey's   1/3 oz. Rum
1/4 oz. Tequila

Hand swirl in glass. Pour over rocks in a pony
glass with a lime twist.

Dangerous Liaisons

Equal parts: Tia Maria & Cointreau
splash of Sour Mix

Shake with ice. Strain into chilled cordial glass.

Day In The Shade

1 oz. Malibu Rum   1 oz. Pineapple Juice
1/2 oz. Cranberry Juice

Shake over ice. Strain into chilled cocktail glass.

DC-9

Equal parts: Sambuca, Rum, Cream & Kahlua

Layer in exact order into a shot glass.

Death By Chocolate

1 oz. Kahlua   1 oz. Chocolate Syrup
1 oz. Vodka
2 scoops Chocolate Ice Cream
1 oz. Dark Crème de Cacao

Blend. Garnish with whipped Cream & cherry.

Deathwish

Equal parts: Grenadine, Wild Turkey, Peppermint
Schnapps, 151 Rum

Layer in exact order into a shot glass.

Deauville Cocktail

1/2 oz. Lemon Juice   1/2 oz. Brandy
1/2 oz. Apple Brandy   1/2 oz. Triple Sec

Shake over ice. Strain into chilled cocktail glass.

Debonair Cocktail

Scotch   1 Lemon twist
1 ounce Original Canton Delicate Liqueur
2 1/2 ounces Oban or Springbank single malt

Stir over ice. Strain into a chilled cocktail glass. Garnish with lemon twist.

 ## Deep Sea

1 oz. Dry Vermouth   1 oz. Gin
2 dashes Pernod   2 dashes Orange Bitters
1 Olive   1 Lemon twist

Combine with ice and shake. Strain and add ice. Garnish with fruit.

 ## Deep Throat

3/4 oz. Vodka   1/4 oz. Tia Maria
Whipped Cream

Build in exact order into a shot glass. Top with whipped cream. No hands should be used to drink this shooter!

Depth Charge

1 oz. Spearmint or Peppermint Schnapps
1/2 glass of Draught Beer

Drop shot into beer. Chug.

Di Saronno Sea Breeze

1 oz. Di Saronno Amaretto
1 oz. Malibu Rum
splash of Cranberry & Pineapple Juice

Build in highball glass with crushed ice.

Diamond Head

1/2 oz. Amaretto   1/4 oz. Drambuie
2 1/2 oz. Light Rum 1 oz. Orange Juice
1 oz. Lime Juice   1 oz. Grapefruit Juice
1 oz. Pineapple Juice 1 dash Grenadine
1 slice Pineapple

Combine with ice and shake. Strain and add ice.

Diamond Jim

1 oz. Rum   1/2 oz. Amaretto
splash of Orange   splash of Cranberry
splash of Pineapple Juice splash of Sour Mix

Shake over ice. Strain into rocks glass.

Die Harder

1 1/2 oz. Curaçao   1 1/2 oz. Rum
1 1/2 oz. Pineapple Juice

Combine with ice and shake. Strain and add ice.

Dimple Doozies

1 oz. Absolut Mandrin   1/2 oz. Peach Schnapps
1/2 oz. Cherry Pucker

Shake over ice and strain.

Dirty Ashtray

1/2 oz. Gin	1/2 oz. Vodka
1/2 oz. Light Rum	1/2 oz. Tequila
1/2 oz. Blue Curaçao	1/2 oz. Grenadine

splash of Pineapple Juice splash of Sour Mix

Shake. Strain into chilled cocktail glass. Garnish with lemon wedge.

Dirty Harry

1 oz. Grand Marnier   1 oz. Tia Maria

Stir over ice. Strain into chilled cocktail glass.

Dirty Martini

1 1/2 oz. Gin   Olive Juice
Dry Vermouth (if desired)

Stir over ice. Strain into chilled cocktail glass.

Dirty Mother

1 1/2 oz. Brandy   1/2 oz. Kahlua
1/2 oz. Cream

Combine with ice and stir.

Dirty Mother II

1 1/2 oz. Brandy   3/4 oz. Kahlua

Combine and add ice.

Disarita Margarita

3 oz. Margarita mix   1/2 cup crushed Ice
1 oz. Jose Cuervo 1800 Tequila
1/2 oz. Di Saronno Amaretto

Blend. Garnish with lime.

Dixie

2 tsp. Dry Vermouth	1 oz. Gin
2 tsp. Pernod	2 dashes Grenadine
1 1/2 oz. Orange Juice	

Combine with ice and shake well. Strain and add ice.

Dizzy Daisy

1 1/4 oz. Vodka   3/4 oz. Crème de Banana
pureed Strawberries   Cream

Blend. Pour over ice in hurricane glass.

Doc's Painless Shot

1 1/2 oz. Mentholmint Schnapps

Combine with ice and stir. Strain and serve straight up.

Dogface

1 oz. Gin   Beer to fill

Drop shot glass with Gin into beer glass.

Double Jack

Equal parts: Jack Daniels & Yukon Jack

Build in shot glass.

Down East Delight

Equal parts: Cranberry, Pineapple & Orange Juice
dash of Simple Syrup

Combine. Serve over ice in a collins glass.
Garnish with cherry.

Down Under

1 oz. Irish Whiskey   *1 oz. Bailey's*
1 oz. Kahlua   *splash of Cream*

Build over ice in a snifter.

Down Under Dreamsickle

6 oz. Orange Juice   *1 splash Rum*
1 splash Soda Water
1 1/2 oz. Bailey's Irish Cream

Blend with ice. Float rum.

Down Under Snowball

1 oz. Light Rum   *1 oz. Peach Schnapps*
1/2 oz. Grenadine   *3 oz. Orange Juice*

Blend with ice.

Downtown

1 oz. Maker's Mark   *7-UP*
1/2 oz. Disaronno Amaretto
splash Sour Mix

Shake vigorously. Serve in collins glass with ice
and top with 7-UP. Garnish with cherry.

Dragon Fire

1/2 oz. Green Crème de Menthe
1 1/2 oz. Pepper Vodka

Combine with ice.

Drambuca

1 oz. Drambuie   *1 oz. Sambuca*

Combine with ice and stir.

Dream Weaver

1 1/2 oz. Crown Royal   *1/2 oz. Light Rum*
Sprite   *Orange Juice*
Grenadine

Fill glass with ice. Add liquor. Evenly mixing OJ
and Sprite fill the glass. Add a splash of grenadine. Garnish with a cherry.

Dreamsicle

1 1/4 oz. Amaretto   *Orange Juice*
Cream

Shake with ice. Serve on the rocks. Strain to
serve up or blend with ice for frozen variation.

Drink & Die

2 oz. Sambuca   *2 oz. Tequila*
4 dash Tabasco

Build in exact order. Pour into shot glass.

Dry Manhattan Cooler

21

1 oz. Dry Vermouth 2 oz. Whiskey
Club Soda to fill 2 tsp. Lemon Juice
2 oz. Orange Juice 2 tsp. Almond Extract

Combine all but club soda with ice. Shake, strain and add soda with ice.

Dubbonet Cocktail

8

1 1/4 oz. Dubbonet 1 1/4 oz. Gin
dash of Bitters

Pour over ice in rocks glass. Garnish with twist.

Duchess

8

1 oz. Dry Vermouth 1 oz. Pernod
1 oz. Sweet Vermouth

Combine with ice and shake. Strain and add ice.

Duck Fart

3

Equal parts: Kahlua, Bailey's & Crown Royal

Build in order into shot glass.

Dynasty

2

1 1/2 oz. Amaretto
1 1/2 oz. Southern Comfort

Shake over ice. Strain into chilled cocktail glass.

Earthquake

1

1 1/2 oz. Tequila 1 tsp. Grenadine
1 quart Strawberry 2 dashes Orange Bitters
1 wedge Lime 3 oz. Ice

Blend until smooth. Garnish with lime wedge.

East India Cocktail

2

1 1/2 oz. Cognac 1 oz. Pineapple Juice
dash Angostura Bitters
1/2 oz. Caraçao or Triple Sec

Shake with ice. Strain into chilled cocktail glass.

East India Cocktail II

2

1 1/2 oz. Brandy 3 dashes Bitters
3 dashes Raspberry Syrup
3 dashes Red Curacao
3 dashes Maraschino Cherry Juice

Combine, shake with cracked ice. Strain and serve with a lemon twist.

Easter Egg

21

1 oz. Rum 1 oz. Apricot Brandy
Pineapple Juice Apple Juice

Blend and serve over ice in collins glass. Garnish with orange slice and cherry.

Easter Egg Shooter

3

Equal parts: Chambord, Tia Maria & Cream

Layer in exact order into a shot glass.

Eight Seconds

4

Equal parts: Jagermeister, Goldshlager, Hot Damn, Rumpleminze

Shake over ice. Strain.

El Diablo

1 1/2 oz. Tequila   1/2 oz. Crème de Casis
1 1/2 tsp. Lime Juice   Ginger Ale to fill
1 Lime twist

Combine all but soda with ice and shake. Strain and add soda and ice. Garnish with fruit.

_____

 Electric Banana

1 1/2 oz. Banana Liqueur   1 oz. Tequila

Layer in exact order.

_____

 Electric Iced Tea

3/4 oz. Rum   3/4 oz. Gin
3/4 oz. Vodka   3/4 oz. Tequila
3/4 oz. Blue Curaçao 3/4 oz. Sour Mix
splash of Sprite

Shake with ice. Pour into hurricane glass. Top with Sprite.

_____

 Electric Kool Aid

1/2 oz. Amaretto   1/2 oz. Cherry Brandy
1/2 oz. Midori   1/2 oz. Southern Comfort
1/2 oz. Triple Sec   1/2 oz. Cranberry Juice
2 dashes Grenadine   1/2 oz. Sour Mix

Combine with ice and shake. Strain and serve straight up.

_____

 Electric Lemonade

1 1/2 oz. Vodka   1/2 oz. Blue Curaçao
2 oz. Sweet & Sour Mix
1 splash Lemon-Lime Soda

Flash blend and garnish with lemon slice.

 Embryo

1 1/4 oz. Peppermint Schnapps
1/2 drop of Grenadine
1 drop of Cream

Pour Schnapps into pony glass. Run drops.

_____

 Emerald Isle

3/4 shot Tullamore Dew   Soda Water
3/4 shot Green Crème de Menthe
2 scoops Vanilla Ice Cream

Blend first 3 ingredients then add soda water. Stir after adding soda water.

_____

 English Coffee

Coffee   Whipped Cream
1/2 oz. each: Kahlua,
Amaretto, Tia Maria &
Dark Crème de Cacao

Combine liqueurs. Fill with coffee. Top with whipped cream.

_____

 English Highball

3/4 oz. Gin   3/4 oz. Brandy
3/4 oz. Sweet Vermouth, Ginger Ale

Build over easy ice into highball glass.

_____

Erection

1 oz. Green Crème de Menthe
Champagne to fill   1 Cherry

Combine and stir.

Eskimo Kiss

Equal parts: *Swiss Chocolate Almond, Cherry Brandy & Amaretto*

Layer in exact order into shot glass. Top with whipped cream.

Everglades Special

1 oz. White Rum   2 tsp. Coffee Liqueur
1 oz. Light Cream
1 oz. White Crème de Cacao

Combine with ice and shake. Strain and add ice.

Eye Opener

1 1/2 oz. Light Rum   1/2 oz. Triple Sec
2 tsp. Pernod   1 tsp. Crème de Cacao
1 Egg Yolk   1 tsp. Sugar

Combine all ingredients in shaker filled with ice. Shake well. Strain into chilled glass.

Face Eraser

1/4 oz. Bailey's   1/4 oz. Kahlua
2 oz. Vodka   1 splash Club Soda

Pour vodka over ice. Add liqueurs. Splash club soda on top.

Fairy Belle

2 tsp. Apricot Brandy   2 oz. Gin
1 tsp. Grenadine   1 Egg White

Combine with ice. Shake and strain. Add ice.

Faliraki Kiss

1 oz. Vodka   1 oz. Blue Curacao
1 oz. Coconut Liqueur   6 oz. Pineapple Juice

Blend with ice until slushy.

Fern Gully Fizz

1 1/2 oz. White Rum   1 oz. Pineapple Juice
1 Tbsp. Lime Juice   1 slice Pineapple
Club Soda to fill
1 1/2 oz. Jamaican Rum

Combine all but soda with ice and shake. Strain and add soda and ice. Garnish with fruit.

Fijian Sunset

1/2 oz. Triple Sec   1 Cherry
1/2 oz. Banana Liqueur   1/2 Banana
1 scoop Ice   ½ oz. Orange Juice
1/2 oz. Pineapple Juice   dash Grenadine
1 Orange wedge

Blend until smooth. Pour. Put Jell-O crystals on rim with orange wedge, cherry and umbrella.

Fireball

3/4 oz. Cinnamon Schnapps
1/4 oz. Cherry Brandy

Layer liqueurs in exact order.

Firecracker 500

1/2 Wild Turkey   1/2 oz. Southern Comfort
1/2 oz. 151 Rum   1 splash Orange Juice
1 splash Sour Mix   1 splash Grenadine
1 Cherry   1/2 oz. Absolut
1/2 oz. Green Chartreuse

Combine with ice and shake. Strain and add ice.

Fish House Punch

2 quarts Rum   1 quart Lemon Juice
1/2 cup Peach Brandy   1 quart Cognac
3/4 pound Sugar

Dissolve sugar in small amount of water, then add lemon juice. Pour mixture over ice. Add Rum, Cognac, Peach Brandy, in exact order. Let stand for 2 hours, stirring occasionally.

Flaming Peter

1 oz. Dry Vermouth   2 tsp. Vodka
1 oz. Peter Heering   2 tsp. Orange Juice

Combine with ice and shake well. Strain and add ice.

Flamingo

1 oz. Beefeater Dry Gin
2 oz. Pineapple Juice
1 oz. Cream of Coconut
1 oz. Sweet & Sour Mix

Blend together with cracked ice until smooth. Strain and serve in chilled glass.

Florida

1/2 oz. Gin   1 tsp. Triple Sec
1 tsp. Kirschwasser   1 tsp. Lemon Juice
1 1/2 oz. Orange Juice   1 Cherry

Combine with ice and shake. Strain and add ice. Garnish with fruit.

Florida Banana Lopez

1 1/2 oz. Vodka   1 cup Ice
4 oz. Orange Juice   1 medium Banana
2 oz. Coco Lopez Cream of Coconut

Mix in blender until smooth.

Florida Fizz!

1/2 oz. Southern Comfort
1 splash Club Soda   2 oz. Orange Juice

Combine all but soda with ice and shake. Strain and add soda and ice.

Florida Punch

3/4 oz. Brandy   1 1/2 oz. Rum
1 1/2 oz. Orange Juice   1 slice Orange
1 1/2 oz. Grapefruit Juice

Combine with ice and shake. Strain and add ice. Garnish with fruit.

Floridian Cocktail

1/2 tsp. Curaçao   3/4 oz. Rye
1 oz. Sweet Vermouth   1 tsp. Amer Picon
2 dashes Orange Bitters   1 tsp. Sugar Syrup

Combine with ice and shake. Strain and add ice.

Flying Kangaroo

1 oz. Vodka   1/4 oz. Galliano
3/4 oz. Coconut Cream   1/2 oz. Cream
1 oz. Rhum Barbancourt
1 1/2 oz. Pineapple Juice

Shake with ice and strain to serve straight up or blend with ice .

Fourth Of July

③

3/4 oz. Grenadine
3/4 oz. Peppermint Schnapps
3/4 oz. Blue Curaçao

Layer in exact order (Grenadine, Peppermint Schnapps, Blue Curaçao).

Frangelico Freeze

⑱

1 1/2 oz. Frangelico Liqueur
4 oz. Vanilla Ice Cream   3-4 Ice Cubes
3 oz. Milk or Half & Half

Blend until smooth and creamy, top with a dollop of whipped cream and cherry.

Free Breeze

⑩

1 oz. Absolut   1/4 oz. Triple Sec
4 splashes Sour Mix   1 wedge Lemon
2 splashes Cranberry Juice

Combine and stir.

Freezer

⑨

1 oz. Brandy
1/2 tsp. Mentholmint Schnapps
1/2 oz. Sweet Vermouth

Combine with ice and stir. Strain and serve straight up.

French Champagne Punch

⑬

1 bottle Champagne   16 oz. Cognac
1 liter White Wine   1 liter Club Soda
8 slices Lemon   8 slices Orange

Combine with ice chunks and garnish with fruit.

French Hooker

⑧

1 oz. Absolut   1 oz. Chambord
1 splash Sour Mix

Combine with ice and stir. Strain and serve straight up.

French Martini

②

1 1/2 oz. Gin   1 dash Scotch
1 Olive

Combine with ice and shake. Strain and serve straight up. Garnish wit fruit.

Frosty Navel

①

1 oz. Peach Schnapps   1 1/2 oz. Cream
1 1/2 oz. Orange Juice   2 oz. Ice
2 scoops Vanilla Ice Cream

Combine with crushed ice and blend until smooth.

Frothy Dawn Cocktail

1 1/2 oz. White Rum 2 tsp. Falemun
1 tsp. Maraschino 1 oz. Orange Juice

Combine with ice and shake Strain and add ice.

Frozen Fruit Daiquiri

1 1/4 oz. Rum Sour Mix
splash Simple Syrup
Fruit, Fruit Juice or Pureed Fruit*

Blend with crushed ice. *Use lime juice for lime,
banana for banana, pureed strawberries & splash
of grenadine for strawberry, etc. Garnish with
whipped cream & lime wedge.

Frozen Grasshopper

3/4 oz. Green Crème de Menthe
3/4 oz. White Crème de Cacao
3 scoops Vanilla Ice Cream

Combine and blend until smooth.

Frozen Lemon Lime

5 oz. Vodka 2 dashes Sprite
1 whole Lemon Ice

Peel lemon add ingredients in blender and mix
well.

Frozen Matador

1 1/2 oz. Sauza Tequila
2 oz. Pineapple Juice 1/2 oz. Grenadine
1/2 oz. Lime Juice

Blend all ingredients with lots of crushed ice and
form a snow cone in a cocktail glass.

Frozen Mint Daiquiri

2 oz. White Rum 2 tsp. Lime Juice
4 leaves Mint 4 oz. Ice
1 1/2 tsp. Sugar Syrup

Combine with crushed ice and blend. Garnish
with mint leaves.

Frozen Pine

1 oz. Canadian Mist 2 oz. Pineapple Juice
1 oz. Grenadine

Blend ingredients in blender until frozen. Pour
into stemmed tulip glasses and garnish with a
cherry.

Frozen Rum Honey

2 oz. 151 Rum 2 tsp. Lemon Juice
1/2 oz. Honey 3 oz. Ice

Combine with crushed ice. Blend until smooth.

Fruit Smoothie

8 oz. Orange Juice 1/2 cup Strawberries
1/2 cup Blueberries 1/2 cup Raspberries
1 Banana 3 oz. Ice

Peel banana and cut into slices. Combine banana
slices with ingredients. Add crushed ice and
blend until smooth.

Fu Manchu

1/2 oz. Triple Sec 1 twist Orange
1/2 oz. White Crème de Menthe
1 1/2 oz. White Rum 1 dash Sugar Syrup
1/2 oz. Rose's Lime Juice

Combine with ice and stir. Strain and garnish
with fruit.

Full In Bed Cocktail

1 oz. Port   4 oz. Apple Juice

Combine with ice and stir.

_____

Funky Monkey

1 oz. Light Rum   4 oz. Orange Juice
1 oz. Crème de Banana

Combine with ice and stir.

_____

Fuzzless Screwdriver

1 1/2 oz. Jubilee Peach Schnapps
1 oz. Vodka   2 oz. Orange Juice

Combine in blender with ice until smooth.

_____

Fuzzy D**k

3/4 oz. Grand Marnier
3/4 oz. Kahlua   Coffee to fill
dash Cream

Combine liqueurs and stir. Fill with coffee and
top with cream.

_____

Fuzzy Navel

1 1/4 oz. Peach Schnapps
1 1/4 oz. Orange Juice

Combine with ice and shake. Strain and serve
straight up.

Gallstone Shooter

1 oz. Crème de Noyaux
1 oz. White Crème de Cacao
1/2 oz. Vodka

Combine with ice and shake. Strain and serve
straight up.

_____

G-Boy

3/4 oz. each Bailey's
Frangelico & Grand Marnier

Shake with ice. Strain into a rocks glass.

_____

Geisha

2 oz. Bourbon   1 oz. Sake
1 1/2 tsp. Lemon Juice
2 tsp. Sugar Syrup   1 Cherry

Combine with ice and shake. Strain and add ice.
Garnish with fruit.

_____

Georgia Margarita

3/4 oz. Peach Schnapps
1 1/2 oz. Tequila   1 oz. Sour Mix

Blend with ice. Garnish with peach slice and
lemon wheel.

_____

Get Laid

1 oz. Vodka
3/4 oz. Raspberry Schnapps
Pineapple Juice to fill
1 splash Cranberry Juice

Combine and stir.

Gibson

2 oz. Gin or Vodka   *dash Dry Vermouth**

Stir with ice. Strain into chilled cocktail glass. Garnish with skewered cocktail onions. *Omit Vermouth if ordered dry.

Gimlet

1 1/2 oz. Gin or Vodka
splash of Lime Juice

Stir with ice. Serve on the rocks in lowball glass or strain into chilled cocktail glass. Garnish with a lime twist.

Gin Aloha

1 tsp. Curaçao   *1 1/2 oz. Gin*
1 Maraschino Cherry
2 dashes Orange Bitters
1/2 oz. Pineapple Juice

Combine with ice and shake. Strain and add ice. Garnish with fruit.

Gin and Lime

1 1/2 oz. Gin   *1 1/2 Tbsp. Lime Juice*
1 twist   *2 tsp. Orange Juice*
1 tsp. Rose's Lime Juice

Combine with ice and shake. Strain and add ice. Garnish with twist.

Gin Aquavit

1 1/2 oz. Gin   *1/2 oz. Aquavit*
1/2 Egg White   *1 tsp. Heavy Cream*
2 tsp. Lemon Juice   *1 tsp. Sugar Syrup*

Combine with ice and shake well. Strain and add ice.

Gin Buck

1 1/4 oz. Gin   *Ginger Ale*

Serve over ice in highball glass. Garnish with lemon wedge.

Gin Cocktail

2 oz. Gin   *2 dashes Bitters*

Stir over ice. Strain into chilled cocktail glass. Garnish with a twist.

Gin Fix

2 1/2 oz. Gin   *1/2 Juice of Lemon*
1 tsp. Powdered Sugar *1 tsp. Water*
1 Lemon Slice

Mix sugar with lemon juice and add water until sugar dissolves. Fill glass with ice and Gin. Stir. Garnish with slice of lemon and serve with straws.

Gin Fizz

1 1/2 oz. Gin   *1 tsp. Sugar*
1/2 Juice of Lemon   *Club Soda to fill*

Shake well with cracked ice all but club soda. Strain into glass over ice. Fill with club soda.

Gin Old Fashioned

1 1/2 oz. Gin   *1 twist Lemon*
3 dashes Angostura Bitters
1/2 tsp. Sugar Syrup

Combine with ice and stir. Garnish with lemon twist.

Gin Punch

8 oz. Gin
1 quart Ginger Ale
2 oz. Lemon Juice
4 oz. Maraschino
1 twist Lemon
2 oz. Sugar Syrup

Combine all but soda and stir. Add ginger ale and ice.

Gin Rickey

1 1/4 oz. Gin
Club Soda
splash of Lime Juice

Serve over ice in highball glass. Top with splash of soda. Garnish with lime wedge.

Ginberry Fizz

2oz. Gin
Club Soda to fill
1 tsp. Raspberry Syrup
2 tsp. Maraschino
1 tsp. Lemon Juice
3 Raspberries

Combine all but soda with ice. Shake, strain, add ice and club soda. Stir and garnish with raspberries.

Gingersnap

1 oz. Ginger Brandy
splash Pineapple Juice
2 splashes Lemonade
1 oz. Vodka

Shake with ice. Pour into a tall glass. Garnish with lemon twist.

Girl Scout Cookie

1/2 oz. Kahlua
1 oz. Peppermint Schnapps
Cream

Hand swirl over ice. Strain into rocks glass.

Godfather

1 1/2 oz. Scotch   3/4 oz. Amaretto

Build over ice in rocks glass.

Godmother

1 1/2 oz. Vodka   3/4 oz. Amaretto

Build over ice in rocks glass.

Golden Cadillac

1 oz. Galliano
3/4 oz. White Crème de Cacao
Cream or Ice Cream

Shake with cream and ice. Strain to serve up, or omit ice and blend with ice cream for frozen variation.

Golden Dawn

1 oz. Apple Brandy
1 oz. Dry Gin
2 dashes Orange Juice
1 oz. Apricot Brandy
1 dash Grenadine

Combine all but grenadine with ice. Shake, strain, add ice and grenadine.

Golden Cream

1 oz. Galliano
Orange Juice
1/2 oz. Triple Sec
Cream or Ice Cream

Shake with ice, Strain to serve up, or omit ice and blend with ice cream for frozen variation.

Golden Margarita

1 1/4 oz. Cuervo
3/4 oz. Grand Marnier
dash each: Sour Mix and Lime Juice

Shake with ice. Serve on rocks or strain into salt rimmed glass. Garnish with lime wedge.

_____

Golden Martini

2 oz. Golden Gin   1/2 oz. Vermouth

Stir over ice. Serve on the rocks or strain into chilled cocktail glass. Garnish with a spear of olives. *For a Dry Martini, omit Vermouth and garnish with a twist.

_____

Golden Screw

1 1/2 oz. Gin
3 dashes Angostura Bitters
2 oz. Orange Juice

Combine with ice and stir.

_____

Goldrush

1/3 Chambord   1/3 Bailey's
1/3 Goldschlager

Layer in order in shot glass.

_____

Golf Martini

2 tsp. Dry Vermouth   1 1/2 oz. Gin
1 Olive
3 dashes Angostura Bitters

Combine and stir. Garnish with olive.

Good & Plenty

Equal parts of: Kahlua and Ouzo

Layer in order in shot glass.

_____

Goom Bay Smash

1 oz. Myers's or Spiced Rum
1 oz. Coconut Rum
1/2 oz. Crème de Banana
splash of Orange Juice and Pineapple Juice

Blend and serve in hurricane glass.

_____

Goombay Splash

1/2 oz. Dark Rum   1/2 oz. Light Rum
1/2 oz. Rum   1/4 oz. Grenadine
1/2 oz. Orange Juice 1/4 oz. Crème de Banana
1/2 oz. Pineapple Juice

Combine with ice and shake. Strain and add ice.

_____

Grand Passion

2 oz. Gin
3 dashes Angostura Bitters
1 oz. Passion Fruit Nectar

Combine with ice and shake. Strain and add ice.

_____

Grand Slam

2 tsp. Dry Vermouth   2 oz. Swedish Punch
2 tsp. Sweet Vermouth

Combine with ice and shake. Strain and add ice.

Grape Crush

Equal parts of: Vodka and Chambord
splash of Sour Mix   dash of 7-Up

Shake. Strain into a lowball glass. Top with 7-UP

Grape Lopez

3 oz. Coco Lopez Cream of Coconut
4 oz. Grape Juice   1 1/2 cups Ice

Mix in blender until smooth.

Grasshopper

1 oz. Green Crème de Menthe
1 oz. White Crème de Cacao
Cream or Ice Cream

Shake with ice. Strain to serve up in flute, or blend with ice cream for frozen variation.

Great Lady

3/4 oz. Bourbon   1 oz. Kahlua
2 oz. Milk   1/2 oz. Honey
1 dash Cinnamon

Mix in blender with ice until smooth. Garnish with cinnamon and cherry.

Great Secret

1 1/2 oz. Gin   2 tsp. Lillet
2 dashes Angostura Bitters
1 twist Orange

Combine with ice and shake. Strain and add ice. Garnish with fruit.

Greek Stinger

1 oz. Anisette   2/3 oz. Galliano

Combine with ice and stir. Strain and serve straight up.

Green Apple

1 oz. Apple Schnapps   dash Lime Juice

Hand swirl over ice. Strain into salt rimmed shot glass.

Green Bay Smash

1 oz. Coconut Rum   1 oz. Midori
1/2 oz. Crème de Banana
Orange Juice   Pineapple Juice

Blend all but Midori and pour over ice in tall glass. Float Midori on top.

Green Genie

Equal parts: Green Chartreuse and Tequila

Hand swirl over ice. Strain into shot glass.

Green Iguana

3/4 oz. Midori   3/4 oz. Tequila
3 oz. Sour Mix

Combine with ice and shake well. Strain and add ice. Garnish with fruit.

Green Sneaker

1 oz. Vodka   1/2 oz. Midori
1/2 oz. Triple Sec   splash of Orange Juice

Hand swirl over ice. Strain into rocks glass.

Green Spider

8

1/2 oz. Green Crème de Menthe
1 1/2 oz. Vodka

Combine with ice and stir.

_____

Gremlin

2

1 1/2 oz. Vodka   3/4 oz. Blue Curaçao
3/4 oz. Rum   splash of Orange Juice

Shake with ice. Strain into chilled cocktail glass.

_____

Grenadine Rickey

10

1 1/2 oz. each of Grenadine and Lime Juice
Soda

Combine juices over ice in highball glass. Add soda. Garnish with lime wedge.

_____

Greyhound

10

1 1/4 oz. Vodka   Grapefruit Juice

Build in highball glass.

_____

Guava Cooler

21

1/2 oz. Maraschino   1 1/2 oz. White Rum
1 oz. Pineapple Juice   1 oz. Sour Mix
1/2 oz. Sugar Syrup
1 1/2 oz. Guava Nectar

Combine with ice and shake. Strain and add ice.

Gumby

3

3/4 oz. Midori   1 1/4 oz. Vodka
3/4 oz. Sour Mix   3/4 oz. Lemon Soda

Combine with ice and shake. Strain and serve straight up.

_____

Gypsy Cocktail

2

1 1/4 oz. each: Gin and Sweet Vermouth

Stir over ice. Strain into chilled glass. Garnish with cherry.

_____

Hairy Navel

10

1 1/4 oz. Vodka   Orange Juice
3/4 oz. Peach Schnapps

Build over ice in a highball glass.

_____

Hammerhead

21

1/2 oz. Light Rum   1/2 oz. Malibu
1/2 oz. Vodka   1/2 oz. Grenadine
2 oz. Orange Juice   1 oz. Pineapple Juice
1/2 oz. Captain Morgan

Combine all but grenadine with ice and stir. Float grenadine on top.

_____

Hangover Cocktail

10

4 Stalks of Celery   2 tsp. of Tabasco Sauce
3 Tbsp. Vinegar   1 Lemon
4 slices of Onion   3 Tbsp. of Sugar
Salt and Pepper to taste
1 large can of Tomato Juice

Mix ingredients in a container, let stand overnight. Strain and serve.

Harbor Lights

3

Equal parts: 151 Rum, Kahlua, Tequila

Layer in Shot glass.

Hard D**k

3

3/4 oz. Vodka   1/2 oz. Frangelico
splash of Soda

Shake with ice. Strain into shot glass.

Harvey Wallbanger

21

1 1/4 oz. Vodka   splash of Galliano
Orange Juice

Pour Vodka and orange juice over ice in collins glass. Top with Galliano.

Hasta La Vista Baby

3

1/8 oz. Amaretto   1/8 oz. B & B
1/8 oz. Triple Sec   1 dash Dry Vermouth
1/2 oz. Vodka   1/2 oz. Jose Cuervo Gold
1/2 oz. Orange Juice   1/2 oz. Pineapple Juice
1/2 oz. Peach Schnapps
1 splash Rose's Lime Juice

Combine with ice and shake. Strain and serve straight up.

Hasty Cocktail

2 1 1/2 oz. Gin
3/4 oz. Dry Vermouth
1 dash of Grenadine & drop of Pernod

Stir with ice. Strain into chilled cocktail glass.

Havana

8

1 oz. Apricot Brandy   1/2 oz. Gin
2 tsp. Swedish Punch   1 dash Lemon Juice

Combine with ice and shake. Strain and add ice.

Havana Bandana

1

2 oz. Bacardi   1 Banana
1/2 oz. Lime Juice   3 oz. Ice
3 dashes Banana Liqueur

Combine (except banana liqueur) and blend.
Float Banana Liqueur on top.

Havana Club

8

1 Tbsp. Dry Vermouth   1 1/2 oz. White Rum

Combine with ice and shake. Strain and add ice.

Havana Cocktail

2

3/4 oz. Rum   dash Lemon Juice
1 1/4 oz. Pineapple Juice

Stir with ice. Strain into chilled cocktail glass.

Hawaiian

3

Equal parts: Vodka, Amaretto & Cranberry Juice

Shake with ice. Strain into shot glass.

Hawaiian Cocktail

2

2 oz. Gin   1/2 oz. Triple Sec
1 splash Pineapple Juice

Shake and strain.

Hawaiian Hooker

1/2 oz. Amaretto
1/2 oz. Southern Comfort
1/4 oz. Grenadine
1 1/2 oz. Pineapple Juice

Combine with ice and shake. Strain and serve straight up.

_____

Hawaiian Snow

1 oz. Bourbon   1 oz. Coffee Liqueur
5 oz. Milk   4 oz. Ice

Combine with crushed ice and blend until smooth. Garnish with orchid.

Head Room

1/4 oz. Crème de Banana,
1/4 oz. Midori   1/2 oz. Bailey's

Layer in order in shot glass.

_____

Head Wind

1 oz. 151 Rum   1 oz. Brandy
1/2 oz. Blue Curaçao   1 oz. Dark Rum
1 oz. Light Rum   1 oz. Vodka
2 oz. Sour Mix   4 oz. Orange Juice
2 oz. Pineapple Juice   1 slice Pineapple

Combine with ice and shake. Strain and add ice. Garnish with fruit.

_____

Heart Throb

1 oz. La Grande Passion
1 1/2 oz. Apple Juice
1/2 oz. Cranberry Juice

Combine with ice and stir.

_____

Heaven

2 oz. Coconut Rum   4 oz. Orange Juice
dash Gin   Whipped Cream
2 scoops Vanilla Ice Cream

Mix in blender. Garnish with whipped cream.

_____

Heavenly Spirits

1/2 oz. Amaretto   1/4 oz. Galliano
1/4 oz. Triple Sec   1 oz. Vodka
2 oz. Orange Juice

Combine with ice and shake. Strain and serve straight up.

6

Hemingway

1 1/2 oz. Pernod   Champagne to fill

Combine and stir.

2

Hennessey Martini

1 3/4 oz. Hennessey
splash of Lemon Juice

Shake with ice. Strain into chilled cocktail glass.
Garnish with lemon twist.

1

Hibiscus
(Three Cocktails)
1/4 cup Brandy or Cognac
3/4 cup Grand Marnier
1/4 cup Lemon juice   1/4 cup Orange Juice
1/4 cup Lime Juice

Combine all ingredients in blender with 2 cups
ice cubes. Blend until ice is partially broken up.
Pour unstrained into 8-oz. cocktail glasses.

2

High Voltage

1 oz. Scotch
3/4 oz. Cointreau or Triple Sec
1/2 juice from Lime or Lemon

Shake with ice. Strain into cocktail glass.

10

Highball

1 1/4 oz. Liquor   Water
Ginger Ale   7-UP

Build with your choice of Liquor in a highball
glass filled with ice.

2

Ho Ho and a Barrel of Rum

1 1/2. oz Old Fashioned Root Beer Schnapps
1 oz. Rum   1 oz. Milk or Cream

Combine in blender with ice until smooth.

2

Honey Bee

1 oz. Jamaican Rum   1/2 oz. Honey
1 1/2 oz. Lemon Juice

Combine with ice and shake. Strain and serve
straight up.

2

Honey Drop

3/4 oz. Bailey's   3/4 oz. Vodka
3/4 oz. Butterscotch Schnapps

Combine with ice and shake well. Strain and
serve straight up.

11

Honeysuckle

1 1/2 oz. Gold Rum   1 tsp. Honey
1 oz. Lime Juice

Combine with ice and shake. Strain and add ice.

8

Hoot Man

1 oz. Scotch   1/2 oz. Lillet
2 tsp. Sweet Vermouth

Combine with ice and shake. Strain and add ice.

♏ (3) Hooter

Equal parts: Vodka, Amaretto, Grenadine & Orange Juice

Shake over ice. Strain into rocks glass.

———————————

♏ (21) Hooty Hoot

3/4 oz. Amaretto
3/4 oz. Peach Schnapps
1 1/2 oz. Vodka
1 1/4 oz. Cranberry Juice
1 1/4 oz. Grapefruit Juice

Combine with ice and stir.

———————————

♏ (8) Hop Frog

1 1/2 oz. Brandy   2 oz. Lime Juice

Combine with ice and shake. Strain and add ice.

———————————

♏ (4) Hot Buttered Rum

1 Lemon Twist   1 Stick of Cinnamon
1 Clove   Boiling Cider
2 oz. Rum   Pat of Butter

In a mug add spices and Rum. Fill with cider & float butter on top.

———————————

♏ (4) Hot Nutty Irishman

3/4 oz. each: Bailey's & Frangelico, Coffee, Whipped Cream

Build in coffee mug. Top with whipped cream. Garnish with a cherry.

♏ (4) Hot Toddie

1 tsp. Sugar   Boiling Water
1 1/4 oz. Brandy Bourbon or choice of Liquor

In a mug, add 1 teaspoon of sugar and liquor. Fill with hot water. Garnish with orange twist.

———————————

♏ (21) Hukilau

1 oz. Jamaican Rum   1 oz. Light Rum
1 oz. Lemon Juice   1 oz. Orgeat Syrup
1 slice of orange   1 cherry

———————————

♏ (18) Hummer

1 oz. each: Kahlua & Rum
2 scoops Ice Cream

Blend with crushed ice. Serve in decorative glass.

———————————

♏ (2) Hummingbird

2 oz. Vodka   1 Banana
1/2 oz. Kahlua   dash Milk
1 oz. Bailey's Irish Cream
dash Strawberry Syrup

Mix in blender until smooth.

———————————

♏ (8) Hunter's Cocktail

1 Tbsp. Cherry Brandy   1 1/2 oz. Rye
1 Cherry

Combine and serve straight up. Garnish with cherry.

Hunters Coffee

1/2 oz. each: Tia Maria & Grand Marnier
Coffee   Whipped Cream

Build in coffee mug. Top with whipped cream.
Garnish with cherry.

Ideal Cocktail

1 oz. Dry Vermouth & Gin
1/4 tsp. Maraschino
1/2 tsp. Grapefruit Juice

Shake with ice. Strain into chilled cocktail glass.
Garnish with cherry.

 ### Hurricane

3/4 oz. each: Rum, Dark Rum, Apricot Brandy
splash Grenadine
Sour Mix

Shake with ice. Serve in hurricane glass. Garnish
with a flag.

Iguana

3/4 oz. Kahlua   3/4 oz. Tequila
3/4 oz. Vodka

Combine with ice and stir.

Ice Pick

1 1/4 oz. Vodka   Iced Tea

Pour over ice in collins glass. Garnish with
lemon wedge.

I'll Fake Manhattan

1 1/2 oz. each: Cranberry Juice & Orange Juice
2 dashes of Orange Bitters
dash of Grenadine and Lemon Juice

Stir over ice. Serve up in chilled cocktail glass.

 ### Icebreaker

2 oz. Tequila   2 tsp. Cointreau
2 oz. Grapefruit Juice   1 Tbsp. Grenadine
4 oz. Ice

Combine with crushed ice. Blend until smooth.

Income Tax Cocktail

1 oz. Dry Gin   1 tsp. Dry Vermouth
1 tsp. Sweet Vermouth
2 dashes Angostura Bitters
1 Tbsp. Orange Juice

Combine with ice. Shake. Strain and add ice.

 ### Iced Rum Coffee

1 1/2 oz. White Rum   1 tsp. Jamaican Rum
6 oz. Coffee   1 tsp. Sugar
2 Tbsp. Whipped Cream

Combine rums and iced coffee and sugar. Fill
glass with ice. Top with whipped cream.

Independence Day Punch

2 quarts Bourbon   8 oz. Lime Juice
16 oz. Pineapple Juice   4 bottles Club Soda

Combine all but soda with ice. Stir. Strain and
add soda and ice.

Indian River

1 tsp. Sweet Vermouth
1 1/2 oz. Whiskey
1 tsp. Raspberry Liqueur
2 tsp. Unsweetened Grapefruit Juice

Combine with ice. Shake. Strain and add ice.

Indian Summer

1 tsp.
2 oz. Apple Schnapps   4 oz. Apple Cider
1 stick Cinnamon

Rim glass with cinnamon. Add Apple Schnapps
and fill remainder with heated apple cider.
Garnish with cinnamon.

Irish Alexander

1 oz. Irish Mist   1 oz. Cream
2 dashes Nutmeg
1 oz. Dark Crème de Cacao

Combine with ice. Shake. Strain and serve
straight up. Top with nutmeg.

Irish Coffee

Fresh Hot Coffee   Fresh Cream
2 tsp. Sugar
1 jigger of Irish Whiskey

Stir into coffee mug.

Irish Dream

1/2 oz. Carolans Irish Cream
1/2 oz. Hazelnut Liqueur
1/2 oz. Dark Crème de Cacao
1 scoop Vanilla Ice Cream

Combine ingredients in a blender with ice. Blend
well. Pour into a collins or parfait glass. Serve
with a straw.

Irish Frog

3/4 oz. Midori
3/4 oz. Chilled Bailey's

Layer into cordial glass.

Irish Headlock

Equal parts: Bailey's, Irish Whiskey, Amaretto
& Brandy

Layer in order into cordial glass.

Irish Laced

1 oz. Irish Mist   Orange wedge
2 splashes Cream
2 splashes Cream of Coconut
3 splashes Pineapple Juice

Combine ingredients with ice. Blend. Garnish
with orange wedge.

Irish Quaalude

Equal parts: Bailey's, Vodka, Frangelico &
White Crème de Cacao

Shake with ice. Strain into shot glass.

Island Iced Tea

dash 151 Rum   1/2 oz. Dark Rum
1 tsp. Falernum   10 oz. Light Rum
2 dashes Lemon Juice   1 cup Tea
1 slice Lemon   1 sprig Mint

Combine all but 151 Rum with ice. Shake. Strain
and add ice. Float 151 Rum on top. Garnish with
lemon and mint.

Island Pleasure

10

1/2 oz Frangelico   2 oz. Cream
1 1/2oz Angostura   Grenadine
1 oz. Cream of Banana

Blend all ingredients with crushed ice. Serve in a 12 oz. glass. Garnish with pineapple slice and cherry.

Island Tea

8

1/2 oz. Vodka   3 oz. Dark Tea
1 oz. Grenadine   1 tsp. Lemon Juice
1 sprig Mint

Combine with ice. Shake. Strain and add ice. Garnish with mint.

Islander Cocktail

1

1 oz. Light Rum   3 oz. Ice
1/2 oz. Orange Curaçao
1/4 oz. Orgeat Syrup
2 dashes Angostura Bitters

Combine ingredients with crushed ice. Blend until smooth.

Isle of Coconut

21

1 1/2 oz. White Rum   1 tsp. Orange Juice
2 tsp. Lime Juice   1 tsp. Sugar Syrup
1 tsp. Lemon Juice
2 tsp. Cream of Coconut

Mix all in blender with 3 oz. crushed ice until smooth. Garnish with slices of coconut.

Isle of Pines

6

1 1/2 oz. Light Rum   5 Mint Leaves
1/2 oz. Lime Juice   3 oz. Ice
1 tsp. Peppermint Schnapps

Combine all ingredients except leaves. Blend.

Italian Coffee

4

1 1/4 oz. Amaretto   Coffee
Whipped Cream

Pour coffee over Amaretto. Top with whipped cream. Garnish with cherry.

Italian Delight

8

1 1/4 oz. Amaretto   1 1/4 oz. Cream
1/2 oz. Orange Juice

Combine with ice. Shake. Strain and add ice.

Italian Iced Tea

8

1 1/4 oz. Sweet Vermouth
Ginger Ale

Serve over ice. Garnish with lemon twist.

Italian Pecker

3

1/4 oz. each: Myers's Rum Cream, Galliano, Tuaca
1/2 oz. Mozart

Shake with ice. Strain into shot glass.

Italian Sombrero

10

1 1/4 oz. Amaretto   Half & Half

Shake with ice. Serve in highball glass.

Italian Spear

8

1 oz. each: Peppermint Schnapps & Amaretto

Build over ice in rocks glass.

_____

Italian Surfer

10

1 oz. each: Amaretto & Malibu
splash Cranberry Juice & Pineapple Juice

Shake with ice. Serve in highball glass.

_____

Italian Surfer with an Attitude

10

1 oz. each: Vodka, Amaretto & Malibu
splash of Cranberry Juice & Pineapple Juice

Shake with ice. Serve in highball glass.

_____

Jack & Jill

3

Equal parts: Jack Daniels & Root Beer Schnapps

Hand swirl with ice. Strain into shot glass.

_____

Jack Collins

8

1 oz. Apple Jack   *splash Club Soda*
2 oz. Sour Mix   *1 slice Orange*
1 Cherry

Combine all but soda with ice. Shake. Strain and add soda and ice. Garnish with fruit.

_____

Jack Off

3

1/2 oz. each: Jack Daniels & Bailey's

Shake with ice. Strain into shot glass.

Jack Rose

2

1 1/2 oz. Apple Brandy
splash of Lime Juice   dash of Grenadine

Shake with ice. Strain into chilled cocktail glass.

_____

Jackhammer

10

1/4 oz. Vodka   Pineapple Juice

Build in highball glass.

_____

Jack-in-the-Box

8

1 1/4 oz. Apple Brandy
3 dashes Angostura Bitters
1 1/2 tsp. Lemon Juice
2 tsp. Pineapple Juice

Combine with ice. Shake. Strain and add ice.

_____

Jacks Martini

2

1 oz. Gin   1 oz. Absolut Citron
1/4 oz. Dry Vermouth

Combine with ice. Stir. Strain and serve straight up.

_____

Jagerita

8

1/2 oz. each: Jagermeister, Cuervo, Cointreau
splash of Lime Juice

Shake and strain into rocks glass.

_____

Jaguar

18

2 oz. Galliano
1 oz. White Crème de Cacao
2 scoops Ice Cream

Blend & Serve. Top with whipped cream.

Jamaica Ginger

2 tsp. 151 Rum	1/2 oz. Jamaican Rum
1 1/2 oz. White Rum	2 tsp. Falenum
2 tsp. Lime Juice	1 slice Pineapple
1 chunk Ginger	splash Ginger Beer

Combine rums, Falenum and juice with ice.
Shake. Strain and add ice. Fill with ginger beer.
Dip pineapple in White Crème de Menthe.
Garnish with pineapple slice and ginger.

Jamaica Glow

1 1/2 oz. Dry Gin	1 tsp. Jamaican Rum
1/2 oz. Red Wine	2 tsp. Orange Juice

Combine with ice. Shake. Strain over crushed
ice. Garnish with lemon wedge.

Jamaica Me Crazy

1/2 oz. each: Amber Rum & Tia Maria, splash
Pineapple Juice

Over ice in highball glass.

Jamaican Banana

1/2 oz. Light Rum
1/2 oz. Crème de Banana
1/2 oz. White Crème de Cacao
1/2 oz. Cream
2 scoops Vanilla Ice Cream

Mix in blender until smooth.

Jamaican Barbados Bomber

1 oz. Myers's Rum	1 oz. Mount Gay Rum
1/2 oz. Triple Sec	dash Lime Juice

Combine with ice. Stir. Strain and serve straight
up.

Jamaican Coffee

1 oz. Tia Maria	3/4 oz. Rum
Coffee	Whipped Cream

Pour coffee over Kahlua & Rum in coffee mug.
Top with whipped cream. Garnish with cherry.

Jamaican Dust

Equal parts: 151 Rum, Tia Maria & Pineapple
Juice

Shake with ice. Strain into shot glass.

Jamaican Egg Cream

1 oz. Gin	dash Club Soda
1 tsp. Lemon Juice	1 oz. Light Cream
1 tsp. Sugar Syrup	
1 1/2 oz. Jamaican Rum	

Combine all but soda with ice. Shake. Strain and
add soda and ice.

Jamaican Hop

1 oz. each: Kahlua
White Cream de Cacao & Cream

Shake over ice. Strain into chilled cocktail glass.

Jamaican Hot
Tea Punch

1 pint Brandy   *1 pint Jamaican Rum*
1 slice Lime   *2 slices Orange*
3 pints Tea   *1 Tbsp. Sugar*
1/2 tsp. Cinnamon.

Combine Brandy, Rum, fruit juices and hot tea in a saucepan. Heat slowly and stir. Add sugar and cinnamon.

Jamaican Lollipop

1 oz. Crème de Banana
1/2 oz. 151 Rum

Combine with ice. Shake. Strain and serve straight up.

Jamaican Shandy

1 bottle Red Stripe Beer
1 pint Ginger Beer

Combine. Stir slowly. Serve over ice.

Jamaican Tennis Beads

1/2 oz. each: Vodka, Malibu Rum, Crème de Banana, Chambord, Pineapple Juice, Half & Half

Shake with ice. Strain into shot glass or serve on the rocks.

Jell-O Shots

Prepare Jell-O according to package with boiling water, let cool a bit. Substitute Vodka for the cold water. Pour into molds and chill. (Note: Use 3/4 cups if you want them firm).

Jelly Bean

Equal parts: Anisette & Blackberry Brandy

Layer into shot glass.

Jelly Donut

1 oz. Chambord   Cream

Layer into shot glass.

Jellyfish

Equal parts: White Crème de Cacao, Amaretto, Bailey's, drop of Grenadine

Shake all but Grenadine. Pour into pony glass. Using a straw drop a little Grenadine in the middle.

Jenny Wallbanger

1/2 oz. Galliano   1 oz. Vodka
1 1/2 oz. Cream   1 1/2 oz. Orange Juice

Combine all but Galliano with ice. Shake. Strain and add ice. Float Galliano on top.

Jezebel

Equal parts: Southern Comfort & Bailey's

Layer into a shot glass.

Jogger

Splash of Lime Juice   Soda

Combine over ice. Serve in highball glass.
Garnish with lime wedge.

_____

John Collins

1 1/4 oz. Bourbon   Sour Mix
Soda

Shake over ice. Pour into a collins glass. Top
with soda. Garnish with orange slice and cherry.

_____

Johnny Appleseed

2 scoops Ice Cream   2 oz. Apple Juice
splash Orange Juice & Soda

Blend with ice until smooth. Serve in champagne
glass.

_____

Johnny Cocktail

1 Tbsp. Curaçao   1 1/2 oz. Sloe Gin
1 tsp. Anisette

Combine with ice. Shake. Strain and add ice.

_____

Jolly Green Giant

Equal parts: Rum, Gin, Tequila, Blue Curaçao
& Galliano

Hand swirl with ice. Strain into a shot glass.

Jolly Rancher

3/4 oz. Vodka
1/4 oz. each: Midori & Peach Schnapps
splash of Cranberry Juice

Shake with ice. Strain into rocks glass or shot
glass.

_____

Jolly Roger

1 oz. Drambuie   1 oz. Light Rum
3 dashes Scotch   dash Club Soda
1/2 oz. Lime Juice

Combine all but soda with ice. Shake. Strain and
add soda and ice.

_____

Just A Kiss

1/4 oz. Amaretto
1/2 oz. Dark Crème de Cacao
1/4 oz. Galliano
1/2 oz. White Crème de Cacao
1/2 oz Cream

Combine with ice. Shake. Strain and serve
straight up.

_____

Kadushi

1 oz. Vodka   2 oz. Coconut Cream
2 oz. Pineapple Juice   1/2 oz. Grenadine
3/4 cup crushed Ice

Blend until smooth. Pour into a chilled collins
glass.

_____

Kahlua Banana

1 1/2 oz. Kahlua   3/4 oz. Rum
2 oz. Pineapple Juice   Ice
2 oz. Cream of Coconut Fresh Banana

Blend together.

Kahlua Colada

1 oz. Kahlua   1/2 oz. Rum
2 oz. Pineapple Juice   1 cup Ice
1 oz. Coco Lopez Cream of Coconut

Blend with ice and serve in a margarita glass.

Kahlua Colada-2

1 1/2 oz. Kahlua
2 oz. Crème of Coconut
2 oz. Pineapple Juice

Add ice and blend.

Kahuna

1/2 oz. 151 Rum   1 oz. Jamaican Rum
1 oz. Dark Rum   1/2 oz. Apricot Liqueur
1 oz. Light Rum   3/4 oz. Lime Juice
1 tsp. Sugar Syrup   1 wedge Pineapple
1 Cherry   3/4 oz. Pineapple Juice

Combine all but 151 Rum with ice. Shake. Strain and add ice. Float 151 Rum on top. Garnish with fruit.

Kalani Boy

1 oz. Light Rum   1 oz. Dark Rum
1/2 oz. 151 Rum   1/2 oz. Guava Juice
1/4 oz. Grenadine   1 oz. Lemon Juice
1/2 oz. Orange Juice
1/2 oz. Passion Fruit Juice
1/2 oz. Pineapple Juice
1 slice Pineapple

Combine all but 151 Rum with ice. Shake. Strain and add crushed ice. Float 151 Rum on top. Garnish with pineapple slice.

Kamikaze

1 oz. Vodka   3/4 oz. Triple Sec
dash of Lime Juice & Sour Mix

Shake with ice. Strain into chilled cocktail glass.

Kandy Kane

3/4 oz. Rumple Minze
1/4 oz. Crème de Noyaux

Layer in shot glass.

Kat's Kiss

1 oz. Crème de Noyaux   1 oz. Bailey's
2 scoops of Ice Cream

Blend. Pour in champagne glass.

Kaytusha Rocket

1 oz. Vodka   1/2 oz. Kahlua
splash Pineapple Juice   dash of Cream

Shake with ice. Strain into chilled cocktail glass.

Kentucky Cocktail

3/4 oz. Bourbon
1 1/2 oz. Pineapple Juice

Shake with ice. Strain into chilled cocktail glass.

Kentucky Colonel

1 1/2 oz. Bourbon   1/2 oz. Benedictine

Shake with ice. Strain into chilled cocktail glass. Garnish with lemon twist.

Keoki Shooter

1/2 oz. each: Hot Coffee, Kahlua, Dark Crème
   de Cacao
1/4 oz. Irish Whiskey or Brandy

Build in cordial glass. Top with whipped cream.

Keuka Cup

6 slices Orange   1 1/2 tsp. Lemon Juice
8 oz. cubed Pineapple   1 Tbsp. Sugar Syrup
1 bottle Champagne

Combine and chill. Add ice before serving.

Key Largo

3/4 oz. Campari   1/4 oz. Triple Sec
splash of Grapefruit Juice & Soda

Build in highball glass. Top with splash of soda.

Key Lime Pie

1 1/2 oz. Licor 43
splash of Lime Juice & Cream

Shake with ice. Strain into shot glass.

Key Wasted

1 oz. Mt. Gay Rum   1/4 oz. Cointreau
Juice from 1/2 fresh Lime
dash of Roses Lime Juice

Shake with ice. Strain into chilled cocktail glass.

Key West Margarita

1 1/2 oz. Tequila   1 oz. Melon Liqueur
1 oz. Piña Colada Mix   1/2 oz. Lime Juice
1/2 oz. Orange Juice   1 dash Grenadine
1/2 cup crushed Ice

Blend until smooth. Pour into a hurricane glass.

Kiddy Cocktail

Sour Mix   splash of Grenadine

Shake with ice. Serve in highball glass. Garnish
with orange wheel and cherry.

King Alphonse

1 oz. Dark Crème de Cacao   Cream

Layer Cream on top of Crème de Cacao in pony
glass. Spear cherry & place on top.

Kioki Coffee

3/4 oz. Brandy   3/4 oz. Kahlua
Coffee   Whipped Cream

Combine Liqueurs, add coffee in mug. Top with
whipped cream. Garnish with a cherry.

Kir

3/4 oz. Crème de Casis   White Wine

Pour Crème de Casis in bottom of wine glass. Fill
with wine. Garnish with a twist.

Kir Royale

3/4 oz. Crème de Casis   Champagne

Pour Crème de Casis in bottom of champagne glass. Fill with champagne. Garnish with a twist.

_____

Kiss In The Dark

3/4 oz. each: Gin, Cherry Brandy & Dry Vermouth

Shake with ice. Strain into chilled cocktail glass.

_____

Kitchen Sink

3/4 oz. Amaretto & Orange Curaçao
dash each of: Orange, Pineapple Juice & Sour Mix

Shake with ice. Strain into chilled cocktail glass.

_____

Kiwi

3/4 oz. Crème de Banana
3/4 oz. Strawberry Schnapps
2 1/2 oz. Orange Juice

Combine with ice. Stir.

_____

Klondike

1 1/2 oz. Apple Jack   Lemon twist
1/2 oz. Dry Vermouth
3 dashes Angostura Bitters

Combine with ice. Stir. Strain. Garnish with cherry.

Knock Out Cocktail

3/4 oz. Gin & Dry Vermouth
1/2 oz. Pernod
1 tsp. White Crème de Menthe

Shake with ice. Strain into chilled cocktail glass. Garnish with cherry.

_____

Koala Bear

1 oz. Crème de Banana
1 oz. Dark Crème de Cacao
2 scoops Vanilla Ice Cream

Blend with ice. Garnish with whipped cream & sprinkle with nutmeg.

_____

Koko Coffee

Coffee   Whipped Cream
Dark Crème de Cacao
1 oz. White Cream de Cacao

Put coffee in mug on top of White Crème de Cacao. Top with whipped cream. Garnish with dribbles of Dark Crème de Cacao.

_____

Kokonut Kamakazi

2 oz. Malibu   1 oz. Pineapple Juice
splash Sour Mix

Combine with ice. Shake. Strain and serve straight up.

_____

Kool-Aid

1/2 oz. each: Amaretto, Vodka & Midori
* splash of Cranberry Juice*

Shake with ice. Strain into chilled cocktail glass or serve as shooter.

Kretchma Cocktail

2

1 oz. each: Vodka & White Crème de Cacao
1/2 oz. Lemon Juice   dash of Grenadine

Shake with ice. Strain into chilled cocktail glass.

L.A. Freeway

3

The spillage bar mat at the end of the night.
Line up shot glasses and pour!

La Grande Affaire

2

1/2 oz. Grand Marnier   2 oz. La Grande Passion

Combine with ice. Shake. Strain and serve
straight up.

Ladies Cocktail

8

1 1/2 oz. Whiskey   1 dash Anisette
1 dash Pernod   1 stick Pineapple
3 dashes Angostura Bitters

Combine with ice. Shake. Strain and add ice.
Garnish with orange wedge.

Lady in Red

21

1 1/2 oz. Malibu Rum   1 1/2 oz. Bailey's
2 oz. Coconut Cream   3/4 cup crushed Ice
2 oz. Fresh Strawberries

Blend until smooth. Pour into a chilled collins
glass.

Laser Beam

10

1/2 oz. Amaretto   1/2 oz. Midori
1/2 oz. Vodka   1 oz. Lemon Soda
1 oz. Orange Juice   1 oz. Sour Mix
1/2 oz. Grand Marnier
1/2 oz. Southern Comfort

Combine with ice and stir.

Latin Lover

8

1 oz. Amaretto   1 oz. Tequila

Combine with ice and stir.

Lava Flow

1

1 oz. Light Rum   1 oz. Jamaican Rum
1 dash Grenadine   1/2 oz. Lemon Juice
1 slice Lemon   1 wedge Pineapple
4 oz. Ice   1 dash Orange Curaçao
1 1/2 oz. Pineapple Juice

Combine with crushed ice. Blend until smooth.

Le Coq D'or

8

1/2 oz. Triple Sec   1 oz. Gin
1/2 oz. Apricot Brandy
1/2 oz. Dry Vermouth

Combine with ice. Shake. Strain over ice.
Garnish with orange wedge.

Leave It To Me

8

2 oz. Gin   1 dash Maraschino
1/4 oz. Lemon Juice   1 tsp. Raspberry Syrup

Combine with ice. Shake. Strain and add ice.

Leeward

2 tsp. Sweet Vermouth   Twist of Lemon
1 1/2 oz. White Rum   2 tsp. Calvados

Combine with ice. Shake. Strain and add ice.

Leg Spreader

1 oz. Galliano   1 oz. Kahlua

Combine with ice. Shake. Strain and serve
straight up.

Lemon Drop I

2 oz. Absolut Citron

Swirl over ice. Serve in chilled cocktail glass with
a sugared lemon wedge.

Lemon Drop II

1 1/2 oz. Vodka   splash of Sour Mix
dash of Lemon Juice

Shake. Strain into chilled sugar rimmed cocktail
glass. Garnish with lemon wedge.

Lemon Squash

Lemon wedges   Soda
splash of Simple Syrup

Muddle lemon with syrup. Add ice. Top with soda.

Lethal Injection

Equal parts: Malibu, Captain Morgan, Bacardi
Black & Crème de Noyaux
splash of Orange & Pineapple Juice

Shake with ice. Strain into chilled rocks glass.

Lethal Weapon

1/2 oz. Peach Schnapps   1 oz. Vodka
splash Cranberry Juice & Lime Juice

Combine with ice. Strain and serve straight up.

Liberty

dash Sugar Syrup   1 Tbsp. Rum
1 1/2 oz. Apple Brandy

Combine with ice. Shake. Strain and add ice.

Liberty Cocktail

1 1/2 oz. Apple Brandy   3/4 oz. Rum
dash of Simple Syrup

Stir with ice. Strain into chilled cocktail glass.

Licorice Stick

1 oz. Vodka
1/2 oz. each: Anisette & Triple Sec

Stir over ice. Strain into rocks glass.

Lifesaver

1 oz. Smirnoff Vodka   1 oz. Triple Sec
2 oz. Orange Juice   2 oz. Pineapple Juice
1/2 tsp. Grenadine

Blend and pour over ice.

Lime Cola

Splash of Lime Juice   Cola

Serve over ice in tall glass. Garnish with lime
wedge.

Lime Cooler

Splash of Lime Juice   Tonic

Serve over ice in tall glass. Garnish with lime wedge.

Lime Daiquiri Freeze

1 1/2 oz. Rum   1 oz. Lime Juice
4 oz. Sour Mix   1 1/2 cups crushed Ice

Blend until smooth. Pour into a hurricane glass.

Lime Freeze

2 scoops Ice Cream   3 oz. Lime Juice

Blend until smooth. Garnish with lime wedge.

Little Devil Cocktail

1 oz. Lemon Juice
3/4 oz. each: Rum & Gin
dash of Triple Sec

Shake with ice. Strain into chilled cocktail glass.

Little Princess Cocktail

1 1/4 oz. each: Rum & Sweet Vermouth

Stir with ice. Strain into chilled cocktail glass.

Lobotomy

1 oz. Vodka   1 oz. Kahlua
1/2 oz. Rum   Soda

Spoon Float / straw.

Lobotomy-2

Equal parts of: Amaretto, Chambord & Pineapple Juice
Champagne

Shake with ice. Strain into shot glass. Top with champagne.

Lola Martini

2 oz. OP Vodka   1/2 oz. Cointreau
1/2 oz. Fresh Lime Juice
1/2 oz. Elderflower Syrup
splash Cranberry Juice
Thin slice Strawberry

Mix in shaker. Strain into a chilled martini glass.

Long Beach

3/4 oz. Rum, Gin, Vodka, Tequila & Triple Sec
splash of Sour Mix & Cranberry Juice

Shake all. Pour in hurricane glass. Garnish with lemon wedge.

Long Island Ice Tea

Sour Mix   splash of Cola
3/4 oz. each: Rum, Gin, Vodka, Tequila & Triple Sec

Shake liquors with Sour Mix. Pour in hurricane glass. Add splash of cola. Garnish with a lemon wedge.

L'Orange Royale

Equal parts: Orange Juice concentrate (thawed)
Grand Marnier   Vodka
dash of Grenadine

Layer in exact order into chilled pony glass.

Louisiana Bayou

Equal parts: Kahlua, Midori & Bailey's

Layer into shot glass.

Luxury Cocktail

2 dashes of Orange Bitters
3 oz. each: Brandy & chilled Champagne

Stir gently in large champagne glass.

Lynchburg Lemonade

1 1/4 oz. Jack Daniels
splash of Triple Sec & Sour Mix
7-UP

Shake with ice. Pour in highball glass. Top with splash of 7-UP.

M & M

Equal parts: Kahlua & Amaretto

Layer into shot glass.

Madras

1 1/4 oz. Vodka
splash of Cranberry & Orange Juice

Build in a highball glass.

Mai Tai

1 1/2 oz. Dark Rum
dash of Grenadine
1/2 oz. each: Orange Curaçao & Crème de Noyaux, Lime Juice

Shake with ice & serve in hurricane glass.

Maiden's Blush Cocktail

3/4 oz. Absinthe substitute (Pernod)
1 1/2 oz. Dry Gin   1 tsp. Grenadine

Shake with ice. Strain into chilled cocktail glass.

Malibu

3/4 oz. Spiced Rum   3/4 oz. Vodka
Orange Juice

Build over ice in highball glass.

Malibu Caribbean Cooler

2 oz. Malibu   1/2 ripe Banana
1/2 scoop Vanilla Ice Cream
1/2 cup crushed Ice

Blend until smooth, serve in a stemmed glass.

Malibu Italian Surfer

1 oz. Malibu Rum
1/2 oz. Di Saronno Amaretto
splash Cranberry & Pineapple Juice

Build over ice in highball glass.

Malibu Orange Colada

1 1/2 oz. Malibu   1 oz. Triple Sec
4 oz. Piña Colada Mix

Blend with ice until smooth.

Manhattan

1 1/2 oz. Whiskey or Bourbon
3/4 oz Sweet Vermouth*
dash of Bitters

Build in rocks glass or stir over ice & strain into chilled cocktail glass to serve up. Garnish with cherry. *Perfect Manhattan use equal parts of sweet & dry up. Garnish with lemon twist.

Margarita

1 1/2 oz. Tequila
3/4 oz. Triple Sec (or Cointreau)
splash Sour Mix   dash Lime Juice

Shake with ice & serve in salt rimmed glass on the rocks or strain to serve up. Add more liquid and blend with ice for frozen. Garnish with lime wedge.

Margarita Madres

1 1/4 oz. Jose Cuervo Gold Tequila
1/2 oz. Cointreau
1 1/2 oz. Sweet & Sour Mix
1 1/2 oz. Orange Juice
1 1/2 oz. Cranberry Juice

Blend with crushed ice. Garnish with a lime.

Martini

2 oz. Gin   1/2 oz. Vermouth*

Stir over ice. Serve on the rocks or strain into chilled Cocktail glass. Garnish with spear of olive. *For Dry Martini, omit Vermouth & garnish with a twist. Vodka may be substituted for a Vodka Martini.

Martinique Punch

2 oz. Rum   wedge of Key Lime
1 tsp. Sugar   Ice

Stir. Serve on rocks glass.

Mat Cocktail

The spillage mat at the end of the night. Line up shot glasses and pour!

Melonball

1 1/2 oz. Melon Liqueur
1 oz. Vodka
splash Orange & Pineapple Juice & or Grapefruit Juice

Build in highball glass.

Memphis Belle

Equal parts: Southern Comfort & Bailey's

Shake over ice. Strain into shot glass.

Merry Widow

1 1/2 oz. each: Gin & Sweet Vermouth
dash each: Pernod & Bitters

Serve over ice in rocks glass or strain into chilled glass. Garnish with lemon twist.

Merry Widow Fizz

1 1/2 oz. Sloe Gin
splash each: Sour Mix, Orange Juice & Soda

Shake Sloe Gin & juices. Pour over ice in tall glass. Add soda to fill.

Mexican Berry

3/4 oz. Chambord   *1/4 oz. Cuervo Gold*

Shake with ice. Strain into sugar frosted shot glass.

Mexican Coffee

3/4 oz. each: Kahlua & Tequila
Coffee   *Whipped Cream*

Pour coffee over liqueurs. Top with whipped cream. Garnish with cherry.

Mexican Grasshopper

3/4 oz. each: Kahlua, White Crème de Cacao, Cream

Shake over ice. Strain into chilled cocktail glass.

Mexican Mist

1 1/2 oz. Sauza Conmemorativo
1 1/2 oz. each of Pineapple, Orange & Cranberry Juice

Serve over ice in tall glass.

Miami Sunset

1 oz. Bourbon   *1/2 oz. Triple Sec*
Orange Juice   *dash Grenadine*

Build over ice in highball glass.

Miami Vice

Cola as needed   *1/2 oz. Chocolate Syrup*
2 oz. each: Cream, Root Beer

Shake all but cola with ice. Top with cola in tall glass.

Midori Colada

2 oz. Midori   *6 oz. Colada Mix*
2 oz. Cream of Coconut
4 oz. Pineapple Juice
1 1/2 cups crushed Ice

Blend until smooth. Pour into a hurricane glass.

Midori Margarita

1 oz. Midori   *1 1/2 oz. Tequila*
1 oz. Sweet & Sour Mix

Blend and pour into salted glass.

Miles of Smiles

1/2 oz. each: Canadian Club
Peppermint Schnapps   Amaretto

Hand swirl with ice. Strain into shot glass.

Milk Punch

1 oz. Whiskey   dash Simple Syrup
Milk

Shake with ice. Serve in highball glass.

Milky Way

1 oz. Cointreau   Cream
1/2 oz. Dark Crème de Cacao

Blend with ice. Pour into balloon glass, top with whipped cream and serve with a cherry.

Millionaire's Margarita

3/4 oz. Grand Marnier 110th or 150th
  Anniversary Blends
2 oz. Ultra-premium 100% Agave Tequila
1 1/2 oz. Fresh Lime Juice
2 cups crushed Ice

Combine in shaker filled with ice. Strain into a chilled margarita glass. Garnish with an orange peel.

Mimosa

Champagne   Orange Juice

In champagne flute, pour 1/4 with orange juice, fill rest with chilled champagne. Garnish with orange wheel.

Mind Eraser

Equal parts: Kahlua & Vodka, splash of Soda

In shot glass, add in order. Serve with a straw.

Mint Julep

2 oz. Bourbon   dash Simple Syrup
Mint

Muddle mint leaves with Simple Syrup, add 1 oz. Bourbon. Fill with crushed ice, add rest of bourbon. Garnish with a sprig of fresh mint.

Missionary

2 oz. Pineapple Juice
1 oz. each: Simple Syrup & Sour Mix

Stir over ice. Garnish with pineapple wedge.

Mist Cream

1 cup Ice in blender   dash of Grenadine
1/2 cup Heavy Cream   1 1/2 oz. Canadian Mist
1/2 oz Coffee Liqueur

Blend ingredients and garnish with cherries.

Mistico Martini

1 oz. each: Jose Cuervo Mistico, Chambord & Sour Mix

Stir with ice. Strain to serve up in chilled cocktail glass.

Mojito

1 1/4 oz. Rum   splash of Soda
dash of Simple Syrup   Mint

Muddle mint leaves with Simple Syrup. Add ice, Rum & top with soda. Garnish with a sprig of fresh mint.

Montego Bay

2 oz. each: Orange Juice & Sour Mix
splash of Grenadine & Sour Mix

Shake with ice. Top with soda. Garnish with a flag.

Montego Margarita

1 1/2 oz. Appleton Estate Rum
1/2 oz. Triple Sec
1 oz. Lemon or Lime Juice
1 scoop crushed Ice

Blend with ice and serve.

Moon Beam

3/4 oz. Amaretto
3/4 oz. White Crème de Cacao

Shake over ice. Serve in rocks glass.

Morning Glory

Champagne   Orange Juice
1/2 oz. Triple Sec

Fill 3/4 champagne flute with chilled champagne. Add orange juice & Triple Sec. Garnish with orange wheel.

Moscow Mule

1 1/2 oz. Vodka   1/2 oz. Lime Juice
4 oz. Ginger Beer

Fill Copper Mug with ice and add ingredients. Give a quick stir.

Mud Slide

1/2 oz. Vodka   1/2 oz. Kahlua
1/2 oz. Bailey's Irish Cream
1 oz. Cream   1/2 cup crushed Ice

Blend and pour into a collins glass.

Muddy River

1 oz. each: Kahlua, Vodka, Bailey's

Stir over ice. Serve in large rocks glass.

Mudslide

1 oz. each: Kahlua, Vodka, Bailey's
2 scoops Vanilla Ice Cream
Oreo Cookie

Break up cookie and blend well. Serve in hurricane glass. Garnish with whipped cream.

Negroni

3/4 oz. each: Campari, Gin & Sweet Vermouth

Stir well with ice. Strain into chilled cocktail glass.

Neutron

2 oz. Vodka   1/2 oz. Midori
dash of Blue Curaçao & 7-UP

Shake with ice. Strain into chilled rocks glass.

Neutron Bomb

1 oz. Beer
1/3 oz. each: Vodka, Rum, Triple Sec,
Amaretto, Sloe Gin & Galliano
splash of Orange Juice

Shake with ice. Strain into chilled cocktail glass.

New York Nut

Dash each: Vodka, Amaretto, Frangelico &
Tia Maria   splash of Cream

Shake with ice. Strain into shot glass.

New York Slammer

3/4 oz. each: Southern Comfort, Amaretto,
Triple Sec, Sloe Gin, Orange Juice

Shake and strain into rocks glass.

Nicholas

Splash each of: Grapefruit, Orange Juice, Sour
Mix, Grenadine

Shake. Serve over ice in highball glass.

Ninja

Equal parts of: Dark Crème de Cacao, Midori
& Frangelico

Layer in order into shot glass.

Nuclear Accelerator

Equal parts of: Vodka, Grand Marnier &
Peppermint Schnapps

Layer in order in shot glass.

Nutcracker

Equal parts of: Vodka, Frangelico & Cream

Hand swirl over ice. Strain into shot glass.

Nutty Colada

3 oz. Amaretto   1/2 oz. Coconut Milk
3 tsp. crushed Pineapple
2 cups crushed Ice

Blend until smooth. Pour into a collins glass.

Nutty Irishman

Equal parts of: Bailey's & Frangelico

Hand swirl over ice. Strain into shot glass.

Nutty Jamaican

1 oz. Myers's Rum Cream
1/2 oz. Frangelico

Hand swirl over ice. Strain into shot glass.

Nymphomanic

1 oz. Captain Morgan's Spiced Rum
1/4 oz. Peach Schnapps
1/4 oz. Malibu Rum

Shake. Swirl into rocks glass.

Oatmeal Cookie

3/4 oz. each: Butterscotch Schnapps &
Bailey's
splash of Jagermeister & Cinnamon Schnapps

Shake over ice. Strain into shot glass. Garnish with skewered raisins.

Old Fashioned

8

2 oz. Whiskey or Bourbon
splash of Simple Syrup, Bitters & Soda

Fill rocks glass with ice. Add Simple Syrup, Bitters, liquor & soda. Garnish with orange slice.

Old Lay

2

1 1/4 oz. Cuervo   3/4 oz. Triple Sec
splash of Lime Juice

Shake with ice. Strain into chilled cocktail glass. Top with a dash of Grenadine.

Orange Blossom

10

1 1/4 oz. Gin   Orange Juice

Pour over ice in highball glass.

Orange Crush

3

Equal parts of: Vodka, Triple Sec & Orange Juice

Shake with ice. Strain into shot glass.

Orange Vodka Delight

18

2 shots Gordon's Orange Vodka
1 12-oz. Can frozen Orange Juice
2 cups Orange-flavored Water
1 cup 7-Up

Pour all ingredients into blender. Fill with ice. Mix until slushy. Pour into frozen long stemmed bowl glass. Place a slice of orange on glass.

Orangeade

Equal parts of Orange Juice & Soda
splash of Simple Syrup

Serve over ice. Garnish with orange slice.

Orgasm

3

3/4 oz. each: Amaretto, Kahlua & Bailey's

Shake over ice. Strain into shot glass.

Outrigger

8

1 oz. Light Rum   1/2 oz. Amaretto
splash of Cranberry Juice & Pineapple Juice

Shake. Strain into chilled cocktail glass. Float 1/2 oz. Rum. Garnish with orange slice.

Pac Man

8

Dash each of: Bitters & Grenadine.
Splash of Lemon Juice, Ginger Ale

Stir all but Ginger Ale over ice. Fill with Ginger Ale. Garnish with orange slice.

Painless

8

3/4 oz. each: Bailey's, Crown Royal, Amaretto

Shake with ice. Serve in rocks glass.

Panama Red

2

1 1/4 oz. Cuervo   3/4 oz. Triple Sec
dash of Sour Mix & Grenadine

Shake over ice. Strain into chilled cocktail glass.

Pancho Villa

3

Equal parts of: Green Chartreuse, Crème de Noyaux, Cuervo & 151 Rum

Layer in order into shot glass.

Panther

3

Equal parts of: Peach Brandy & White Crème de Menthe

Hand swirl over ice. Strain into shot glass.

Passionate Screw

18

2 oz. Passoa   1/2 oz. Vodka
2 oz. Orange Juice

Pour Passoa and Vodka directly into a glass. Fill to the top with orange juice.

Peace in Ireland

3

Equal parts of: Irish Mist and Bailey's

Shake with ice. Strain into shot glass.

Peach Bunny

2

3/4 oz. Peach Brandy   Cream
3/4 oz. White Crème de Cacao

Shake with ice to serve up in chilled cocktail glass.

Peach Delight

8

1/2 oz. Peach Schnapps   1/4 oz. Vodka
1/4 oz. Amaretto
splash of Cranberry Juice

Shake with ice. Serve on the rocks in lowball glass.

Peach Passionate Potion

18

3 oz. Vodka   3 oz. Champagne
3 oz. Peach Schnapps   2 cups Ice
10 slices canned Peaches

Blend until smooth. Pour into a hurricane glass.

Peach Slingshot

3

Equal parts of: Peach Schnapps, Gin & Sour Mix dash of Grenadine

Shake with ice. Strain into shot glass.

Peaches and Cream

3

Equal parts of: Peach Schnapps & Cream dash of 151 Rum

Layer in order in shot glass.

Peanut Butter & Jelly

Equal parts of: Frangelico, Chambord & Cream

Shake with ice. Strain into shot glass.

Peppermint Pattie

1/2 oz. Kahlua   1/4 oz. Vodka
3/4 oz. Peppermint Schnapps
1/4 oz. Dark Crème de Cacao

Shake with ice. Strain into shot glass.

Pearl Harbor

Equal parts of: Vodka, Midori & Pineapple Juice

Shake with ice. Strain into chilled cocktail glass.

Piece Of Ass

1/2 oz. Amaretto   1/2 oz. Sour Mix
1/2 oz. Southern Comfort

Shake with ice strain into a shot glass.

Pearl Necklace

Equal parts of: Vodka, White Crème de Cacao
splash of Cream

Shake with ice. Strain into chilled cocktail glass.

Piña Colada

1 1/4 oz. Rum, splash Cream of Coconut &
Pineapple Juice

Shake with ice. Serve in hurricane glass.
Or
Blend with ice cream for frozen variation.
Garnish with fresh pineapple wedge. Top with whipped cream if frozen.

Pearl Necklace-2

8 oz. Butterscotch Schnapps
4 oz. Bailey's Irish Cream
1 lump Whipped Cream

Place alcohol in blender and fill with ice. Blend until smooth. Pour into glass and top with whipped cream.

Pine Cone

1 oz. Southern Comfort 1 oz. Amaretto
Pineapple Juice

Shake. Pour over ice in rocks glass.

Pearls and Lace

2 oz. each of: Orange Soda, Cola, Root Beer &
7-UP
splash of Lemonade

Combine with ice in hurricane glass.

Pineapple Bomb

1 oz. Southern Comfort
1/2 oz. Amaretto   splash Pineapple Juice

Shake with ice. Strain into shot glass.

Pink Almond

1 oz. Whiskey   3/4 oz. Crème de Noyaux
3/4 oz. Amaretto   splash of Sour Mix

Shake. Pour over ice in rocks glass.

Pink Gin

Splash of Bitters   Gin

Revolve splash of Bitters in chilled cocktail glass until coated. Fill with chilled gin.

Pink Lady

1 1/2 oz. Gin   Cream
Dash of Grenadine

Shake into a champagne flute.

Pink Lassie

1 scoop of Vanilla Ice Cream
2 oz. Cranberry Juice
1 oz. each of: Pineapple Juice & Simple Syrup
splash of Soda

Blend until smooth. Serve in champagne flute.

Pink Lemonade

1 oz. Vodka or Bacardi Limon
3/4 oz. Triple Sec   splash of Sour Mix
Cranberry Juice   7-UP

Shake over ice. Serve up or on the rocks.

Pink Panther

3/4 oz Lemon Juice   3/4 oz. Cream
1 1/4 oz. Bacardi Light-Dry Rum
1/2 oz. Major Peters' Grenadine

Mix in a shaker or blender with ice and strain into a cocktail glass.

Pink Squirrel

Cream   1 oz. Crème de Noyaux
3/4 oz. White Crème de Cacao

Shake over ice. Strain into champagne flute.

Pink Thong

28 Ice Cubes   1 Tbsp. Lime Juice
3/4 cup Grenadine   3 oz. Gin
1/2 bottle Piña Colada Mix
1 1/2 cups Sweet & Sour Mix

Blend until smooth. Serve in a margarita glass.

Planters Punch

1 1/2 oz. Rum   3/4 oz. Triple Sec
splash of Sour Mix   Pineapple Juice
Orange Juice   dash of Grenadine
Dark Rum

Shake. Pour over ice in hurricane glass. Float dark rum on top. Garnish with orange slice.

PMS

Equal parts of: Cranberry & Orange Juice

Serve over ice in highball glass.

Poinsettia

2 oz. Champagne   1/4 oz. Triple Sec
splash of Cranberry Juice

Combine in champagne glass. Garnish with twist.

 Pony's Neck

Dash of Lime Juice   2 dashes of Bitters
Ginger Ale

Combine over ice. Garnish with lemon wheel.

 Pousse Café

Equal parts of: Sloe Gin, Anisette, Green Crème de Menthe, Blackberry Brandy

Layer into shot glass.

 Pousse Platter

Equal parts of: Kahlua, Cream, White Crème de Cacao, Amaretto

Shake. Strain into chilled cocktail glass. Serve on the rocks in highball glass.

Prairie Oyster

Olive Oil   1 Egg Yolk
1 Tbsp. Ketchup   White Vinegar
dash of Worcestershire Sauce
Salt & Pepper

Rinse glass with oil & discard excess oil. Add rest of ingredients being careful not to break the yolk. Serve with a glass of water.

 Presbyterian

1 1/2 oz. Bourbon
splash of Club Soda & Ginger Ale

Build in highball glass. Garnish with lemon twist.

 Puppy's Nose

Equal parts of: Peppermint Schnapps, Tia Maria & Bailey's

Layer Schnapps & Tia Maria. Float Bailey's in shot glass.

 Purple Haze

Equal parts of: Vodka, Chambord
dash of Sour Mix & Cranberry Juice

Shake with ice. Strain into shot glass.

 Purple Hooter

Equal parts of: Vodka, Chambord & Sour Mix, splash 7-UP

Shake with ice. Strain into shot glass. Top with 7-Up.

Purple Nurple

1/2 oz. Tequila   1/4 oz. Blue Curaçao
1/4 oz. Sloe Gin

Hand swirl over ice. Strain into shot glass.

Purple Rain

1 1/2 oz. Vodka
splash each of: Blue Curaçao & Cranberry Juice

Hand swirl over ice. Strain into shot glass.

Purple Rain-2

1 oz. Vodka   1/2 oz. Blue Curaçao
2 1/2 oz. Pineapple Juice

Fill tulip glass with ice, add ingredients. Pour all into blender. Blend until smooth   Pour into glass.

Pushup

1 1/4 oz. Vodka   Orange Juice
splash Grenadine & Cream

Shake. Strain into cocktail glass or blend with ice cream for frozen variation.

Quaalude

Equal parts of: Bailey's, Grand Marnier, Vodka

Stir over ice. Serve as shot or on the rocks.

Quarter Deck Cocktail

1 1/2 oz. Rum, splash of Dry Sherry & Lime Juice

Stir over ice. Strain into chilled cocktail glass.

Rain Forest

1 oz. White Rum   1 oz. Melon Liqueur
1 oz. Passion Fruit   1 cup crushed Ice
1 tsp. Cream of Coconut

Blend until smooth. Pour into a tall glass.

Ramos Gin Fizz

2 oz. Gin   2 oz. Cream
Egg White   Club Soda
1/2 oz. Fresh Lime Juice
2 drops Orange Blossom Water
1 tsp. Powdered Sugar
1/2 oz. Fresh Lemon Juice

Put in blender with cracked ice. Put in highball glass. Add a splash of club soda. Garnish with orange slice.

Raspberry Cream

1 oz. Vodka   1 oz. Chambord
Cream

Build over ice in rocks glass.

Raspberry Grenade

Equal parts of: Peach Schnapps, Vodka, Chambord, Lime Juice

Stir over ice. Strain into pony glass.

Raspberry Iced Tea

1/2 oz. Each of Gin, Vodka, Light Rum, Tequila
splash of Sour Mix   1/2 oz. Chambord

Shake. Strain into chilled cocktail glass or serve on the rocks. Float 1/2 oz. Chambord.

Raspberry Kiss

Equal parts of: Chambord, Kahlua & Cream

Shake with ice. Strain into shot glass.

Raspberry Zinger

1 oz. Chambord   1 oz. Vodka
splash of Grenadine & Orange Juice

Shake with ice. Strain into chilled cocktail glass.

Rattlesnake

3 parts Amaretto   2 parts Kahlua
1 part Cream

Layer in shot glass.

Red Death

1 oz. Vodka   dash Lime Juice
splash Orange Juice
3/4 oz. each: Amaretto, Triple Sec, Southern
Comfort & Sloe Gin

Shake with ice. Pour into highball glass.

Red Headed Slut

Equal parts of: Chambord, Crown Royal &
Southern Comfort

Shake. Strain into chilled cocktail glass.

Red Hot

1 oz. Cinnamon Schnapps
2 drops Tabasco Sauce

Stir in shot glass.

Red Snapper

Equal parts of: Crown Royal, Peach Schnapps &
Cranberry Juice

Shake with ice. Strain into chilled rocks or cocktail glass.

Rhum Barbancourt Freeze

1 oz. Triple Sec   1 oz. Grapefruit Juice
2 oz. Orange Juice   1/2 oz. Lime Juice
1/3 cup Ice Cubes
2 oz. Rhum Barbancourt

Combine ingredients in blender. Blend until
smooth about 30 seconds. Pour into glass.
Garnish with orange wedge.

Ricky Martin

1 1/2 oz. Midori   2 cups Ice
1 1/2 oz. Orange Stolichnaya
2 oz. Piña Colada Mix
1 slice Orange or Honeydew Melon

Blend ingredients well. Pour into a hurricane
glass. Garnish with fruit.

Ritz Pick Me Up

1 oz. Cognac   1 oz. Triple Sec
4 oz. Orange Juice   Brut Champagne

Mix Cognac, Triple Sec and Orange Juice with ice
cubes in goblet. Fill with chilled champagne.

Rob Roy

1 1/2 oz. Scotch   1/2 oz. Sweet Vermouth*
(Dash of Bitters if desired)

Build over ice in rocks glass or stir & strain into
chilled cocktail glass to serve up. Garnish with
cherry. *For a Perfect variation, use equal parts
of Sweet & Dry Vermouth. Garnish with twist.
Use only Dry Vermouth for dry version.

Rock Lobster

1 oz. Chambord   1 oz. Crown Royal
Cranberry Juice

Shake over ice. Strain into chilled cocktail glass.

_____

Rocket Fuel

Equal parts of: Rumple Minze & 151 Rum

Layer into shot glass.

_____

Root Beer Float

1 oz. Vodka   3/4 oz. Galliano
Cream   Splash of Coke

Shake over ice. Pour into highball glass.

_____

Root Beer Slam

1 1/2 oz. Vodka   1 oz. Galliano
splash of Sour Mix & Coke

Shake over ice. Strain into chilled cocktail glass.

_____

Rose Marie's Punch

2 oz. Rum, dash Grenadine
4 oz. each: Pineapple & Grapefruit Juice

Stir. Serve on rocks glass.

_____

Rosie's Special

Equal parts of: Tea & Orange Juice, splash of Soda

Combine over ice. Garnish with cherry.

Rosy Pippin

4 oz. Apple Juice   Ginger Ale
splash of Grenadine & Sour Mix

Shake all with ice. Top with Ginger Ale. Garnish with apple slice.

_____

Roxanne

3/4 oz. each of: Vodka & Peach Schnapps
1/2 oz. Amaretto
splash of Cranberry & Orange Juice

Shake with ice. Strain into small rocks glass.

_____

Roy Rogers

Splash of Grenadine   Cola

Combine over ice. Garnish with flag.

_____

Royal Peach

1 oz. Crown Royal   1/2 oz. Peach Schnapps
splash of Sour Mix

Shake all ingredients with ice. Strain into chilled cocktail glass. Serve on the rocks. Garnish with cherry.

_____

Rum Nut

1 oz. Rum   1/2 oz. Kahlua
Cream of Coconut

Shake over ice. Pour into highball glass, or blend with ice cream for frozen variation.

Rum Runner

1 oz. Rum   splash of Pineapple Juice
Crème de Banana   Orange Juice
dash Grenadine
1/2 oz. each: Blackberry Brandy

Shake. Serve on the rocks in highball glass. Float a bit of dark rum on top.

Rum Yum

1 oz. Bailey's Original Irish Cream
1 oz. Malibu Rum   1 oz. Cream or Milk

Blend with ice.

Rumball

1 oz. Bacardi Rum   3/4 oz. Midori
splash of Orange Juice

Shake with ice. Strain into chilled cocktail glass.

Russian Bear

1 oz. Vodka   Cream
1/2 oz. Cream of Coconut

Shake. Serve on the rocks.

Russian Quaalude

Equal parts of: Bailey's, Frangelico, Vodka

Stir over ice. Serve as shot or on the rocks.

Russian Roulette

2 parts Gin   1 part Kahlua

Float Kahlua over Gin in cocktail glass. When Kahlua sinks, drink!

Rusty Nail

1 oz. Scotch   1 oz. Drambuie

Build. Serve on the rocks.

Saginaw Snooze

3 oz. each of: Apple & Cranberry Juice
1 tsp. Honey

Heat and garnish with lemon slice & cinnamon stick.

Salty Dog

1 1/4 oz. Gin   Grapefruit Juice

Pour in highball glass rimmed with salt, over ice.

San Francisco

2 dashes of Grenadine   Soda
Equal parts of: Pineapple Juice, Orange Juice, Grapefruit Juice, Sour Mix

Shake all but soda with ice. Strain into goblet. Top with soda.

Sangria

1 Tbsp. Sugar   1 Orange
1 Lemon   1 Lime
1 qt. Club Soda
1 large bottle of Dry Red or White Wine
(Optional additions are: 1 oz. Brandy, 1 oz. Triple Sec, Pineapple slices or Maraschino cherries)

Thinly slice fruits. Combine with wine, sugar & options. Refrigerate overnight. Mix with Club Soda just before serving.

Sangrita

21

1 cup Tomato Juice	1 cup Orange Juice
1/4 cup Lime Juice	2 tsp. Tabasco
2 tsp. Minced Onion	Celery Salt
Cracked Pepper	seasoned Salt to taste
2 tsp. Worcestershire Sauce	

Shake. Strain. Refrigerate.

Santa Claus Is Coming To Town

19

Equal parts of: Rumple Minze, Cinnamon Schnapps, Midori, Whipped Cream

Serve in chilled champagne saucer. Top with whipped cream.

Sauza La Bamba

2

3/4 oz. Sauza Conmemorativo
3/4 oz. Frangelico Liqueur
1/2 oz. Orange Juice   1/2 Banana

Blend with ice.

Sauzaliky

10

1 oz. Tequila	splash of Orange Juice
dash of Lemon Juice	1/2 of a Banana

Blend with crushed ice. Serve in highball glass.

Sazerac

8

Whiskey	Pernod
Peychaud's Bitters	Sugar

Swirl Pernod in chilled old fashioned glass to coat. Dissolve sugar & add a couple dashes of bitters to taste. Fill with Whiskey. Garnish with a twist. Traditionally served neat.

Scarlet O'Hara

10

1 1/4 oz. Southern Comfort
Cranberry Juice

Serve over ice in highball glass. Garnish with lime wedge.

Schnookie Brookie

18

1 scoop of Ice Cream
3 oz. each: Orange Juice & Soda

Blend until smooth. Garnish with cherry.

Scooby Snack

10

Equal parts of: Midori & Malibu Rum
splash of Pineapple Juice
Half & Half

Shake all ingredients with ice. Pour into tumbler.

Scorpion

10

1 oz. Brandy	1 oz. Rum
3 oz. Pineapple Juice	dash of Grenadine

Serve over ice in highball glass.

Scotch Smoothie

18

1 oz. Coco Lopez Cream of Coconut
1 1/4 oz. Scotch
1/2 oz. Bailey's Irish Cream
1/2 oz. Almond Liqueur
2 scoops Vanilla Ice Cream

Blend with crushed ice.

Screaming Orgasm

Equal parts: Bailey's, Vodka, Kahlua*

Stir over ice. Strain into rocks glass. *Amaretto can be substituted for another variation.

 ## Screwball

1 1/4 oz. Whiskey   Orange Juice

Serve over ice in highball glass.

Screwdriver

1 1/4 oz. Vodka   Orange Juice

Serve over ice in highball glass.

 ## Seabreeze

1 1/4 oz. Vodka   Grapefruit Juice
Cranberry Juice

Serve over ice in highball glass.

 ## Seahawker

Equal parts of: Blue Curaçao, Vodka & Midori

Layer in order into shot glass.

 ## Separator

1 1/4 oz. Brandy   1 oz. Kahlua
splash of Cream

Shake. Serve over ice in highball glass.

 ## Sex In Faliraki

1 oz. Vodka   1 oz. Peach Liqueur
3 oz. Pineapple Juice   3 oz. Orange Juice
2 cups Crushed Ice

Blend until smooth. Serve in a hurricane glass.

Sex On The Beach

1 oz. Vodka
3/4 oz. each: Chambord & Peach Schnapps
splashes of Pineapple, Orange and Cranberry Juices

Shake with ice. Serve in collins glass.

Sex With An Alligator

Equal parts of: Midori, Malibu Rum, Pineapple Juice, Jagermeister

Shake and strain into chilled cocktail glass. Drop a drizzle of Chambord & let fall to the bottom. Float a thin layer of Jagermeister on top.

 ## Shady Lady

1 oz. Tequila   1 oz. Melon Liqueur
4 oz. Grapefruit Juice

Serve over ice in highball glass. Garnish with a lime twist & cherry.

 ## Shandy

Beer   7-UP

Pour beer in mug, add 7-UP to taste.

 ## Shipwrecked

1 1/2 oz. Bailey's   3/4 cup crushed Ice
1 1/2 oz. Banana Liqueur
1 1/2 oz. Piña Colada Mix
1 scoop Vanilla Ice Cream

Blend until smooth. Serve in a stemmed goblet.

 ## Shirley Temple

Splash of Grenadine   7-UP

Pour Grenadine over highball glass of 7-UP. Garnish with a flag.

 ## Shogun

1/2 oz. Midori   1 1/4 oz. Vodka

Build in shot glass.

 ## Shotgun

Equal parts of: Absolut Citron, Grand Marnier, Lime Juice

Serve over ice in old fashioned glass.

Sicilian Kiss

1 1/2 oz. Southern Comfort   3/4 oz. Amaretto

Pour over ice in rocks glass.

Side Car

1 oz. Brandy   1/2 oz. Triple Sec
splash of Sour Mix

Shake with ice. Serve on the rocks or strain to serve in sugar frosted chilled cocktail glass.

Silent Monk

1 oz. Benedictine   1/2 oz. Triple Sec
splash of Cream

Shake with ice. Strain into rocks glass.

Silk Panty

1 oz. each: Peach Schnapps, Vodka, Cranberry Juice

Stir over ice. Serve in chilled cocktail glass.

Silver Bullet

1 1/2 oz. Gin   splash Scotch

Shake or stir with ice to serve on the rocks or strain to serve up.

Simply Bonkers

Equal parts of: Chambord, Rum & Cream

Shake with ice. Strain into rocks glass.

Singapore Sling

1 1/4 oz. Gin   dash of Grenadine
Sour Mix   Soda
Cherry Brandy

Shake Gin, Grenadine & Sour Mix. Pour in highball glass. Add splash of soda. Float Cherry
Brandy on top. Garnish with orange slice and
cherry.

Sit On My Face

*Equal parts of: Blackberry Brandy, Amaretto,
Triple Sec, Lime Juice*

Layer in pony glass.

Skip and Go Naked

1 oz. Gin   dash of Grenadine
splash of Sour Mix & Draft Beer

Shake over ice. Strain into rocks glass.

Skittle

1/2 oz. Vodka   1/2 oz. Cranberry Juice
1/2 oz. Sour Mix   dash of Grenadine
1/4 oz. Crème de Banana

Shake over ice. Strain into shot glass.

Slalom

1 part Absolut Vodka   1 tsp. Heavy Cream
1 part White Cream de Cacao
1 part Romana Sambuca

Combine in blender with ice. Strain into chilled
cocktail glass.

Slippery Dick

Equal parts of: Peppermint Schnapps & Amaretto

Layer in shot glass.

Slippery Knob

1 1/2 oz. Gin   splash of Grand Marnier

Shake or stir with ice to serve on the rocks.

Slippery Nipple

1 oz. Sambuca   1/2 oz. Vodka
1/2 oz. Irish Cream Liqueur

Put into a chilled shot glass in the order given.

Slippery Nipple-2

Equal parts of: Sambuca & Bailey's

Layer in shot glass.

Sloe Gin Fizz

1 1/4 oz. Sloe Gin   Sour Mix
splash of Soda

Shake. Pour in highball glass. Add splash of
soda. Garnish with orange slice and cherry.

Slow Comfortable Screw

3/4 each: Sloe Gin, Vodka, Southern Comfort & splash of Orange Juice

Shake. Pour in highball glass. Garnish with orange slice and cherry.

Slow Comfortable Screw Up Against the Wall

3/4 oz. each: Sloe Gin, Vodka, Southern Comfort & Galliano
splash of Orange Juice

Shake. Pour in highball glass. Garnish with orange slice and cherry.

Slow Screw

1 oz. Vodka   1/2 oz. Sloe Gin
splash of Orange Juice

Pour over ice in highball glass.

Smith & Kerns

1 1/4 oz. Kahlua   Cream
splash of Soda

Shake Kahlua & cream. Pour over ice in highball glass. Add splash of soda.

Smoopie

1 oz. CicÛn   1/2 oz. Skyy Citrus
1/2 oz. Finlandia Lime   4 oz. Cranberry Juice
splash 7-Up   dash Grenadine
1 packet Sugar

Fill 10 oz. glass with ice, add liquors, sugar and cranberry juice. Shake. Add splash 7-Up and dash Grenadine. Garnish with a cherry.

Smooth Screw

1/2 oz. Tia Maria   1/2 oz. Myers's Rum
1 1/2 oz. Pineapple Juice

Shake with ice. Float 1/2 oz. Barbadian Rum

Snake Bite

1 oz. VO
3/4 oz. Peppermint Schnapps

Hand swirl over ice. Strain into shot glass.

Snowshoe

Equal parts of: Peppermint Schnapps & Brandy

Hand swirl in snifter.

Sombrero

1 1/4 oz. Kahlua   Cream

Shake with ice. Serve in highball glass.

Son of a Peach

1 1/4 oz. Peach Brandy   Sour Mix
Pineapple Juice

Blend with crushed ice until smooth. Serve in hurricane glass.

Sonoma Nouveau

Soda   Cranberry Juice
5 oz. Alcohol Free White Wine

Pour wine over ice. Splash soda to almost fill. Float cranberry juice. Garnish with a twist.

South Paw

Equal parts of: Brandy, Orange Juice, 7-UP

Build in order over ice in highball glass.

___

Southern Hurricane

splash Grenadine   Lemon-Lime Soda
2 cups Ice
1 1/2 oz. Southern Comfort

Combine Southern Comfort and grenadine in a hurricane glass over ice. Fill with lemon-lime soda. Garnish with lime and orange slices.

___

Southern Sparkler

Grapefruit Juice   Pineapple Juice
Soda
1 1/4 oz. Southern Comfort

Shake with ice. Pour in collins glass. Garnish with orange slice and cherry.

___

Southern Suicide

3/4 oz. Jack Daniel's   1/2 oz. Orange Juice
1/4 oz. 7-UP   1/4 oz. Grenadine
3/4 oz. Southern Comfort

Shake with ice. Strain into shot glass.

___

Spanish Coffee

1/2 oz. Tia Maria   1/2 oz. Rum
Coffee   Whipped Cream

Build in coffee mug. Top with whipped cream. Garnish with cherry.

Spritzer

Choice of Wine   Soda

Fill collins glass with ice. Fill 3/4 with wine, fill rest with soda. Garnish with a twist.

___

St. Thomas Lemonade

2 oz. Whiskey   splash of Sour Mix
dash of Grenadine & Soda.

Shake over ice. Pour in collins glass. Top with soda. Garnish with lemon wedge.

___

Star Wars

Equal parts of: Amaretto, Triple Sec, Southern Comfort & Grenadine

Shake with ice. Strain into shot glass.

___

Stinger

1 1/2 oz. Brandy
1/2 oz. White Crème de Menthe

Build over ice in rocks glass.

___

Stone Sour

1 1/4 oz. Whiskey
splash each: Orange Juice & Sour Mix

Shake over ice in highball glass. Garnish with cherry.

___

Storm Cloud

1 oz. Amaretto (or Kahlua)
1/2 oz. 151 Rum   2 drops Cream

Swirl over ice. Strain into shot glass. Drop cream in shot using a straw.

Strawberry Banana Rum Dumb

2 oz. Rum	2 oz. Strawberry Puree
1 oz. Orange Juice	1 oz. Pineapple Juice
4 oz. Ice	2 oz. Whipped Cream
1 Fresh Banana	

Blend until smooth. Pour into a hurricane glass. Top with more whipped cream.

Strawberry Colada

Equal parts of: fresh or frozen Strawberries, Cream of Coconut, Pineapple Juice

Blend with ice until smooth. Serve in hurricane glass. Garnish with a flag.

Strawberry Daiquiri

1 oz. White Rum	1/2 oz. Lime Juice
1/2 cup crushed Ice	1 tsp. Powdered Sugar
1 oz Strawberries	
1/2 oz. Strawberry Schnapps	

Blend until smooth. Pour into a cocktail glass.

Strawberry Daiquiri-2

1 1/2 oz. Rum	dash Grenadine

splash each of: Fresh or frozen Strawberries & Sour Mix

Blend with crushed ice. Garnish with whipped cream.

Strawberry Margarita

1 oz. Tequila	1/2 oz. Triple Sec
Sour Mix	dash of Grenadine

splash each: fresh or frozen Strawberries

Blend with crushed ice. Serve in sugar frosted hurricane glass. Garnish with lime wedge.

Strawberry Orangeana

3 oz. Orange Juice & fresh or frozen Strawberries
1 Banana

Blend with ice until smooth. Garnish with fresh fruit.

Strawberry Smash

1 oz. Light Rum	1/2 oz. 151 Rum
1 oz. Sour Mix	1 cup Strawberries
1 Banana	
1 oz. Wildberry Schnapps	

Blend with crushed ice. Serve in hurricane glass. Garnish with fresh fruit.

Sunset Cooler

4 oz. Cranberry Juice	2 1/2 oz. Orange Juice
splash of Lemon Juice	Ginger Ale

Blend juice with ice until smooth. Top with Ginger Ale.

Sunset Margarita

1 oz. Tequila	1/2 oz. Triple Sec
1/2 oz. Blackberry Brandy	
3 oz. Orange Juice	

Coat bottom of margarita glass with blackberry brandy. Blend remaining ingredients. Pour over brandy.

Swampwater

1 1/4 oz. Green Chartreuse, Pineapple Juice, Lime Juice

Build over ice in highball glass.

Sweet Martini

1 1/2 oz. Gin
splash of Sweet Vermouth

Shake with ice to serve on the rocks; or strain to serve in chilled cocktail glass.

Sweet Peach

1 oz. Amaretto   3/4 oz. Peach Schnapps
1/2 oz. Orange Juice

Shake over ice. Strain into shot glass.

Sweet Tart

1 oz. Vodka
dash each of: Chambord, Lime Juice & Pineapple Juice

Shake with ice. Strain into shot glass.

Swiss Coffee

Coffee   Whipped Cream
1/2 oz. Peppermint Schnapps
1/2 oz. Dark Crème de Cacao

Build in coffee mug. Top with whipped cream.

Swiss Lemonade

1 oz. Absolut Citron   Sour Mix
splash each: Cranberry Juice & 7-UP

Shake Citron & sour mix with ice. Pour into highball glass. Add splash of cranberry juice & 7-UP.

T.K.O.

Equal parts of: Tequila, Kahlua & Ouzo

Shake over ice. Strain into cocktail glass.

Taboo

splash Triple Sec   1/2 oz. Sour Mix
1 1/2 oz. chilled Finlandia Pineapple Vodka
1/2 oz. Cranberry Juice

Blend with crushed ice. Serve in a tall glass. Garnish with a pineapple wedge.

Tequila Sunrise

1 1/2 oz. Tequila, Orange Juice, Grenadine

Pour Tequila & orange juice in collins glass over ice. Trickle Grenadine on top.

Tequini

1 1/2 oz. Tequila   splash of Dry Vermouth

Shake with ice to serve on the rocks; or strain to serve up in chilled cocktail glass.

Test Tube Baby

1 oz. Vodka   1/2 oz. Sambuca
drop of Cream

Combine Vodka & Sambuca in large shot glass. Place straw in cream, place finger over end, place straw in bottom of glass, release finger.

Texas Sweat

Equal parts of: Grenadine, Green Crème de Menthe, Cuervo & Rum

Layer in order into shot glass.

The Twist

3/4 oz. Absolut Vodka   Orange Sherbet
1/2 oz. White Crème de Menthe

Blend. Pour into champagne glass.

The White Cap

1 cup Ice Cubes   Half & Half
1 1/2 oz. Southern Comfort
1 1/2 oz Crème de Cacao

Pour first 3 ingredients into blender. Add half & half until ice cubes are covered. Blend until foamy.

Tia Rumba

Equal parts of: Tia Maria & Rum

Shake over ice. Strain into chilled cocktail glass. Garnish with coffee bean.

Tidal Wave

Equal parts of: 151 Rum, Captain Morgan & Vodka, splash of Sour Mix & Cranberry Juice

Shake over ice. Strain into shot glass.

Tie Me to the Bedpost

1/2 oz. each of: Midori, Absolut Citron, Malibu Rum
splash of Sour Mix

Shake with ice. Strain into chilled cocktail glass.

Tiki Rush

1 oz. Vodka   8 oz. Ice Blue Kool-Aid
1 oz. Peppermint Schnapps

Mix Vodka and Schnapps. Stir with a swizzle stick. Add Ice Blue Kool-Aid, stir again. Pour into a beer mug. Garnish with a parasol and straw.

Toasted Almond

1 oz. Amaretto   1 oz. Kahlua
Cream

Shake with ice. Pour into chilled collins glass.

Tom Collins

Juice of I Lemon   2 drops of Oil of Orange
Juice of 1/2 Lime   1 oz. Dry Gin
Soda Water
1 level tsp. Powdered Sugar

Mix sugar, lemon juice and oil of orange in a tall glass. Add lime juice and Gin, stir well. Put in two medium lumps of ice. Fill to the top with soda water. Stir and serve.

Tomakazi

1 1/4 oz. Gin   1 1/4 oz. Vodka
splash of Lime Juice & Sour Mix

Shake over ice. Strain into chilled cocktail glass.

Tomato Cooler

Tomato Juice
splash of Lemon Juice & Tonic

Combine lemon & tomato juice in tall glass. Top with tonic. Garnish with lemon wedge.

 ## Toots

Ice Cream   2 oz. Orange Soda
1 scoop each of: Orange Sherbet & Chocolate

Blend until smooth. Top with whipped cream & orange wedge.

Tootsie Roll

1 1/4 oz. Dark Crème de Cacao
splash of Orange Juice & Cream

Shake with ice. Pour into highball glass.

 ## Tornado

1 1/2 oz. Ciclûn   1/2 oz. Raspberry Vodka
3 oz. Lemonade

Serve in a large goblet over ice and garnish with a lemon twist.

Toxic Waste

1/2 oz. each: Southern Comfort, Midori & Stoli
splash of Cranberry Juice
dash of Sour Mix

Shake over ice. Strain into chilled cocktail glass.

Traffic Light

Equal parts of: Sloe Gin, Crème de Banana, Green Crème de Menthe

Layer in exact order into shot glass.

 ## Transfusion

3 oz. Grape Juice   6 oz. Ginger Ale
splash of Lime Juice

Combine over ice in highball glass. Garnish with lime wedge.

Trifecta

1/2 oz. each Crème de Banana, Bailey's, 151 Rum
dash of Cream

Shake over ice. Strain into chilled cocktail glass.

Trinity

Equal parts of: Peach Schnapps, Apricot Brandy, Grand Marnier

Build over ice in rocks glass.

 ## Tropical Passion

1 oz. Alize   1 oz. Midori
3 oz. Pineapple Juice   1 oz. Orange Juice

Blend. Garnish with pineapple wedge.

Tropical Storm

1 oz. Light Rum   1/2 oz. Banana Liqueur
2 oz. Orange Juice   1 splash Grenadine
1/2 cup crushed Ice   1 sliced Banana
1 splash Pineapple Juice

Blend until smooth. Pour into a hurricane glass.

T-Shot

Equal parts of: White Crème de Cacao, Tia Maria, Bailey's & Cream

Layer in order into Shot glass.

Ulanda Cocktail

1 1/2 oz. Gin   3/4 oz. Triple Sec
1/4 tsp. Pernod

Shake over ice. Strain. Serve in chilled cocktail glass.

Unfuzzy Navel

3 oz. Orange Juice   dash of Grenadine
1 fresh Peach or Nectarine

Blend with ice until smooth.

Union Jack Cocktail

1 1/2 oz. Gin   3/4 oz. Crème de Yvette
1/2 tsp. Grenadine

Shake over ice. Strain. Serve in chilled cocktail glass.

Urine Sample

Equal parts of: Mt. Gay Rum, Malibu, Amaretto, Orange & Pineapple Juices

Hand swirl over ice. Strain into rocks glass.

V.O. Breeze

Equal parts of: Grenadine, Peppermint Schnapps, V.O.

Layer in exact order in shot glass.

Valencia Cocktail

splash of Orange Juice   2 dashes Orange Bitters
1 1/2 oz. Apricot Brandy

Shake over ice. Strain. Serve in chilled cocktail glass.

Vampire

1 1/4 oz. Vodka   3/4 oz. Chambord
splash of Cranberry Juice

Shake with ice into rocks glass.

Van Vleet

3 oz. Rum
1 oz. each of: Maple Syrup & Lemon Juice

Shake over ice. Pour in an old fashioned glass.

Vanderbilt Cocktail

1 1/2 oz. Brandy   3/4 oz. Cherry Brandy
1 tsp. Simple Syrup   2 dashes of Bitters

Stir with ice. Pour in chilled cocktail glass.

Vell Amic

1 oz. each: Gin, Dubonnet, Grand Marnier

Stir with ice. Pour in chilled cocktail glass. Garnish with cherry.

Velvet Hammer

1 1/2 oz. Vodka   splash of Cream
1/2 oz. White Crème de Cacao

Shake with ice. Serve on the rocks.

Vermont Vigor

1 1/2 oz. Gin   1 oz. Lemon Juice
1/2 oz. Maple Syrup

Shake with ice to serve on the rocks or strain to serve straight up.

Vermouth Casis

Soda   1 1/2 oz. Dry Vermouth
3/4 oz. Crème de Casis

Stir Vermouth & Casis in highball glass, add soda & stir again.

Vesper

2 oz. Gin   1 oz. Vodka
splash of Lillet

Shake with ice to serve on the rocks or strain to serve straight up. Garnish with lemon twist.

Vesuvio

1 oz. Light Rum   1/2 oz. Sweet Vermouth

Shake with ice to serve on the rocks or strain to serve straight up.

Veteran

2 oz. Dark Rum   1/2 oz. Cherry Brandy
Serve in old fashioned glass with ice.

Vicious Sid

1 1/2 oz. Light Rum   1/2 oz. Triple Sec
1 oz. Lemon Juice   1 dash Bitters
1/2 oz. Southern Comfort

Shake. Serve in an old fashioned glass.

Victor

1 1/2 oz. Gin   1/2 oz. Sweet Vermouth
1/2 oz. Brandy

Shake. Serve in chilled cocktail glass.

Victory Collins

1 1/4 oz. Vodka
splash Sour Mix & Grape Juice

Shake with ice. Pour into collins glass. Garnish with orange wheel.

Virgin Mary

6 oz. Tomato Juice   Celery Salt to taste
dash each of Worsterschire, Tabasco, Lime Juice,
Salt & Pepper

Mix all with ice. Garnish with celery stalk.

Vodka 7

1 1/4 oz. Vodka
splash 7-UP & Lime Juice

Pour Vodka & lime juice into collins glass. Add lime wedge & fill with 7-UP.

Vodka Collins

1 1/4 oz. Vodka   Sour Mix
splash Soda

Shake Vodka & Sour Mix with ice. Pour into collins glass. Add splash of soda. Garnish with orange slice.

Vodka Collins Freeze

1 1/2 oz. Vodka   4 oz. Sour Mix
1 1/2 cups crushed Ice

Blend until smooth. Pour into a hurricane glass.

Vodka Gimlet

1 1/2 oz. Vodka   splash of Lime Juice

Stir over ice. Strain into chilled cocktail glass. Garnish with lemon wedge.

Vodka Martini

2 oz. Vodka   1/2 oz. Vermouth*

Shake or stir over ice. Serve on the rocks or strain into chilled cocktail glass. Garnish with a spear of olive. *For a Dry Martini, omit Vermouth & garnish with a twist.

Voodoo Shooter

Equal parts of: Tia Maria, Myers's Rum Cream & 151 Rum

Layer in exact order into shot glass.

Wallick Cocktail

1 1/4 oz. each: Gin & Dry Vermouth
1 tsp. Curaçao

Stir with ice. Strain into chilled cocktail glass.

Wallis Blue

1 1/4 oz. each: Gin & Triple Sec
splash of Lime Juice

Sugar frost a rocks glass. Fill with ice & pour ingredients.

Ward Eight

2 oz. Rye Whiskey   dash of Grenadine
splash of fresh Lime and Lemon Juices

Shake well with ice. Pour into goblet. Garnish with lemon wedge.

Warm Blonde

Equal parts of: Southern Comfort & Amaretto

Layer in shot glass.

Warm Fuzzy

Equal parts of: Peach Schnapps & Blue Curaçao

Pour over ice into rocks glass.

Washington Cocktail

1 1/2 oz. Dry Vermouth 3/4 oz. Brandy
2 dashes of Bitters   dash of Simple Syrup

Stir over ice. Strain into chilled cocktail glass.

Watermelon

1/2 oz. Southern Comfort   1/2 oz. Amaretto
Orange Juice

OR

1/2 oz. Vodka   1/2 oz. Midori
Cranberry Juice

Shake over ice. Strain. Serve in shot glass.

Webster Cocktail

1 oz. Gin   splash Lime Juice
1/2 oz. each: Dry Vermouth & Apricot Brandy

Shake with ice. Strain. Serve in chilled cocktail glass.

Wedding Belle Cocktail

3/4 oz. each: Dubonnet & Gin
splash Cherry Brandy & Orange Juice

Shake with ice. Strain. Serve in chilled cocktail glass.

Wedding Cake

3/4 oz. Gin   3/4 oz. Amaretto
splash of Orange Juice, Pineapple Juice, Cream

Blend with ice. Serve in highball glass.

_____

Weep No More

1 1/2 oz. each: Cognac & Dubonnet
splash Lime Juice   dash Cherry Liqueur

Blend with ice. Serve in chilled cocktail glass.

_____

Wench

Equal parts of: Amaretto & Captain Morgan Rum

Shake with ice. Strain into shot glass.

_____

Werewolf

1 oz. each: Drambuie & Bourbon

Serve with ice in rocks glass.

_____

Western Rose

1 oz. Gin   1/4 tsp. Lemon Juice
1/2 oz. each: Apricot Brandy & Dry Vermouth

Shake with ice. Strain into chilled cocktail glass.

_____

What Me Worry?

Glass of Non-Alcoholic Beer
splash of Tomato Juice or Bloody Mary Mix

Combine in mug. Garnish with lime wedge.

Whip Cocktail

1 1/2 oz. Brandy   1 tsp. Triple Sec
1/4 tsp. Anisette
1/2 oz. each: Sweet & Dry Vermouth

Stir with ice. Strain into chilled cocktail glass.

_____

Whipster

Equal parts of: Dark Crème de Cacao, Apricot Brandy & Triple Sec

Layer in shot glass.

_____

Whiskey Cocktail

2 oz. Whiskey   1 tsp. Simple Syrup
dash of Bitters

Stir over ice. Strain into chilled cocktail glass.
Garnish with cherry

_____

Whiskey Flip

1 1/2 oz. Whiskey   2 tsp. Light Cream
1 tsp. Powdered Sugar   1 Egg
Nutmeg

Shake all ingredients (except nutmeg) with ice.
Strain into flip glass. Sprinkle nutmeg on top.

_____

Whiskey Sour

1 1/2 oz. Whiskey   Sour Mix

Blend with ice. Serve on the rocks, or strain to
serve up in a cocktail. Garnish with an orange slice.

_____

White Cap

4 oz. Chambord   Cream as needed

Pour Chambord into cordial glass. Pour dash of
cream (poured over back of spoon) on top.

White Heart

1/2 oz. Sambuca 2 oz. Cream
1/2 oz. White Crème de Cacao

Blend with ice. Strain to serve up in chilled cocktail glass.

White Lion

1 1/2 oz. Light Rum Juice of 1/2 Lemon
1/2 tsp. Grenadine 1 tsp. Powdered Sugar
2 dashes Bitters

Blend with ice. Strain to serve up in chilled cocktail glass.

White Russian

1 1/4 oz. Vodka 1 oz. Kahlua
splash of Cream

Shake. Serve over ice in rocks glass

White Sands

1 splash Triple Sec 1 cup crushed Ice
1 scoop Vanilla Ice Cream
1/2 oz. Malibu Coconut Rum
1 oz. Vodka

Blend until smooth. Pour into a collins glass.

White Spider

1/2 oz. each: White Crème de Menthe, White Crème de Cacao

Layer in shot glass.

White Way Cocktail

1 1/4 oz. Gin
3/4 oz. White Crème de Menthe

Shake with ice. Strain into chilled cocktail glass.

Why Not?

1 oz. each: Apricot Brandy & Gin
1/2 oz. Dry Vermouth 1 dash Lemon Juice

Shake with ice. Strain into chilled cocktail glass.

Widow Woods Nightcap

2 oz. Scotch 4 oz. Milk
1/2 oz. Dark Crème de Cacao

Shake with ice. Strain into chilled cocktail glass.

Widow's Kiss

1 oz. Brandy 1/2 oz. Benedictine
1/2 oz. Yellow Chartreuse
1 dash Bitters

Shake with ice. Strain into chilled cocktail glass. Garnish with strawberry.

Wildberry Angel

2 oz. Gordon's Wildberry Vodka
1 oz. Crème de Cassis
12 oz. Can frozen Pink Lemonade

Blend with ice until slushy. Pour into frozen long stemmed bowl glass. Place a strawberry over glass rim.

Will Rogers

1 1/2 oz. Gin 1/2 oz. Dry Vermouth
1 dash Triple Sec splash of Orange Juice

Shake with ice. Strain into chilled cocktail glass.

Windex

Equal parts of: Vodka, Triple Sec, Blue Curaçao, Sour Mix

Serve on the rocks in highball glass.

Windsurfer

Equal parts of Kahlua, Triple Sec, Yukon Jack

Layer in shot glass.

Wine Cooler

Choice of Wine   7-UP

Fill collins glass with ice. Fill 3/4 with wine, fill rest with 7-UP. Garnish with lemon twist.

Woo Woo

1 oz. Peach Schnapps   1 oz. Vodka
splash Cranberry Juice

Shake with ice. Strain into chilled cocktail glass. Serve on the rocks in a highball glass.

Woodward Cocktail

1 1/2 oz. Scotch   1/2 oz. Dry Vermouth
1 Tbsp. Grapefruit Juice

Shake with ice. Strain into chilled cocktail glass.

Xango

1 1/2 oz. Rum   1/2 oz. Triple Sec
splash of Grapefruit Juice

Shake over ice. Strain into chilled cocktail glass.

Xaviera

1/2 oz. each of: Amaretto Kahlua & Triple Sec
1 1/2 oz. Cream

Shake over ice. Strain to serve up into chilled cocktail glass.

Xeres

2 oz. Dry Sherry   dash Bitters

Stir over ice. Strain to serve up in chilled cocktail glass.

XYZ

1 oz. Rum   1/2 oz. Triple Sec
splash Sour Mix

Shake over ice. Strain. Serve up in chilled cocktail glass.

Yale Cocktail

1 1/2 oz. Gin   1/2 oz. Dry Vermouth
1 tsp. Crème de Yvette or Blue Curaçao
dash Bitters

Stir with ice. Strain into chilled cocktail glass.

Yashmak

3/4 oz. Whiskey   3/4 oz. Dry Vermouth
splash of Campari

Shake with ice. Pour into collins glass.

Yellow Bird

1 oz. each: Rum, Galliano, Crème de Banana
splash of Orange Juice & Pineapple Juice
dash of Lime Juice

Blend with ice. Pour into collins or hurricane glass.

Yellow Fever

21

1 1/2 oz. Vodka   Lemonade to fill

Pour into collins glass. Garnish with lemon wedge.

Yellow Parrot

2

3/4 oz. each: Apricot Brandy, Anisette, Yellow Chartreuse

Stir with ice. Strain into chilled cocktail glass.

Yellow Submarine

10

1 1/2 oz. Rum   1 oz. Orange Curaçao
splash Sour Mix

Shake with ice. Pour into highball glass.

Z Street Slammer

8

1 1/4 oz. Myers's Rum
1/4 oz. Grenadine
3/4 oz. each: Crème de Banana & Pineapple Juice

Shake with ice. Strain into rocks glass.

Z-28

3

Equal parts of: White Crème de Menthe, Crème de Banana, Tequila

Layer in shot glass.

Zambodian Shooter

2

Equal parts of: Vodka, Blackberry Brandy, Pineapple Juice

Shake with ice. Strain into chilled cocktail glass.

Zapata

7

1/2 oz. Campari   1 oz. Tequila
1 Orange

Combine juice of orange with other ingredients. Add ice and shake well. Strain and serve straight up in a goblet.

Zaza

2

1 1/2 oz. Gin   3/4 oz. Dubonnet

Stir over ice. Serve in chilled cocktail glass. Garnish with orange twist.

Zero Mist

2

2 oz. Green Crème de Menthe   1 oz. Water

Combine ingredients and chill in freezer for one hour or until almost frozen. Serve in chilled cocktail glass.

Zipper

3

Equal parts of: Grand Marnier, Tequila, Irish Cream

Layer in shot glass.

Zipper Head

8

1 oz. each of: 7-UP, Vodka, Chambord

Layer in rocks glass with ice. Serve with straw.

Zombie

21

3/4 oz. Light Rum   3/4 oz. Dark Rum
3/4 oz. Gold Rum   1/2 oz. Cherry Brandy
1 oz. Sweetened Lemon Juice

Blend the Rums and lemon juice together with ice. Strain into collins glass. Garnish with cherry.

INDEX

INDEX

INDEX

INDEX

INDEX

INDEX

INDEX

· Product Order Form ·

If you would like next year's calendar or additional copies of this year's calendar, or copies of our books, please make a copy of this order form. Send check or money order to our address below. If you would like to place an order by credit card, you may call us at 954-680-1771. Minimum orders for credit cards, $25.00. Please order early, quantity is limited.

	PRICE	QUANTITY	TOTAL
CALENDARS			
Key West Calendar (12x12 inches with over 40 pictures)	$9.95	_____	_____
BOOKS			
Florida Keys/Key West (32 Pages, over 100 pictures)	$5.95	_____	_____
(Text in English, French, Spanish and German, 7x10 inches)			
Key West/Florida Keys (48 Pages)	$8.95	_____	_____
(Coffee Table Book with over 60 pictures)			
Florida Address Book (28 Pages)	$3.95	_____	_____
(16 beautiful pictures, address index, 5x7 inches)			
Florida Book (80 Pages, over 145 pictures)	$9.95	_____	_____
(Text in English, French, Spanish and German, 8x11 inches)			
American Lighthouses (32 Pages, over 120 pictures)	$5.95	_____	_____
(7x10 inches with all color pictures)			
Don't Stop The Party (Over 120 pages)	$9.95	_____	_____
(A complete guide to Tropical Drink Recipes from the Florida Keys)			
SCREEN SAVERS			
American Lighthouses (70 pictures, wallpaper and sound)	$12.95	_____	_____
(For Windows™ 95, 98, Me, 2000, XP)			
Key West & The Florida Keys (75 pictures)	$12.95	_____	_____
(Wallpaper and sound, for Windows™ 95, 98, Me, 2000, XP)			

Prices subject to change. SHIPPING: Most shipping is handled by UPS or the Post Office. Please list street address. All orders are not necessarily shipped together. All items are satisfaction guaranteed or your money will be promtly refunded if returned in good condition within 30 days.

SHIPPING CHARGES: If your order totals:
$ 0.00 - $ 9.99 — $ 4.00
$10.00 - $19.99 — $ 5.00
$20.00 - $35.00 — $ 6.50
$35.01 - $50.00 — $ 8.50
$50.01 - $75.00 — $10.00
over $75.00 — $12.00
Overseas orders add $10.00 to above prices.

Total All Items _____

FL Residents add 6% Sales Tax _____

Shipping Charges _____

Total Due _____

Visa / Mastercard

_____   _____   _____
Card Number   Exp. Date   Signature

Please make sure that your billing address of the credit card is the same as your shipping address!

NAME: _____

STREET ADDRESS: _____

_____

CITY: _____

STATE: _____   ZIP: _____

PHONE: _____

We also accept Checks or Money Orders payable to:

Pro Publishing, Inc.
P.O. Box 266601
Weston, Fl. 33326
954-680-1771